HOW ^{TO} HELP

YOUR CHILD

EXCEL ^{IN} MATH

An A to Z Survival Guide

By

BRITA IMMERGUT

CAREER PRESS

FRANKLIN LAKES, NJ

The original dictionary was completed in 1994 with COPE (College Opportunity to Prepare for Employment) funds.

HOW TO HELP YOUR CHILD EXCEL IN MATH
Cover design by Foster & Foster
Edited by Jodi L. Brandon
Typeset by Eileen Munson
Printed in the U.S.A. by Book-mart Press

To order this title, please call toll-free 1-800-CAREER-1 (NJ and Canada: 201-848-0310) to order using VISA or MasterCard, or for further information on books from Career Press.

The Career Press, Inc., 3 Tice Road, PO Box 687, Franklin Lakes, NJ 07417
www.careerpress.com

Library of Congress Cataloging-in-Publication Data

Immergut, Brita.
    How to help your child excel in math : an A to Z survival guide / by Brita Immergut.
        p. cm.
    ISBN 1-56414-528-X (paper)
    1. Mathematics—Study and teaching. I. Title.

QA11 .I434 2001
510—dc21

00-050713

This book
is dedicated
to my daughters
Ellen, Eva, and Karin
so that they will be able to help
their children excel in mathematics.

C O N T E N T S

This book is for parents who help their children with math problems but who have forgotten most of the math they studied years ago or who don't know math vocabulary. It is also for people who claim that when they open a math book they feel that a wall has come down in front of them. They have "math anxiety": the feeling they will never be able to understand math and that it is useless to try. To help you—whether you are a parent, student, or anyone who needs to strengthen his or her math skills—I have written this book to be a handy and quick way to refresh your memory and to reassure yourself that you *can* help with math homework or help someone to prepare for a math test.

This is how the Dictionary works:

At the beginning of the book there is a Glossary of basic terms that will be used throughout the book to help you refresh your memory. Then, for more detail with examples and practice problems, look at the entries in the text itself.

Following the Glossary there are three appendices: Numbers, Translations, and Properties. These are topics many people have difficulties with, and so it is convenient to have them in a separate place.

The alphabetized Dictionary is arranged as follows: Each topic word is followed by a definition, examples and, if appropriate, practice problems. Most definitions contain several cross-references (that is, words that can be found elsewhere). These are written in caps. It may not be necessary to look up all of these, but the cross-references will help you understand a definition if you are not familiar with the language of math.

There are usually only a few examples for each entry; if you feel you need more exercises, you should refer to a textbook on the appropriate level.

Many math words have several meanings, depending on the math area involved. For example, "median" has one meaning in statistics but a different one in geometry. These different meanings are clearly stated with definitions and examples.

Word problems are difficult for many people. So-called "templates" are introduced in this book to help you sort out the information given in a word problem. Once you understand the information, you will be able to write the equation necessary to solve the problem.

Do not worry if your calculator gives results (especially on compound interest) that are different from mine. That is because calculators round differently.

I hope that this "survival guide" will serve its purpose and help you to become more comfortable with math.

—Brita Immergut
April 2001

Absolute value: The magnitude (size) of a number. It has no sign before it and is always positive. The *value* of 3 is always +3.

Algorithm: A rule to follow step by step in order to solve a certain problem.

Approximation: A rough estimate of a value. For example, 3.05 is approximately equal to 3 and 3.05 × 2.10 is approximately equal to 6. An approximation can be written as 3.05 ≈ 3.

Average: The term usually refers to the arithmetic mean, which is the total of all data divided by the number of data. The average of 3, 5, and 7 is 5 (15 ÷ 3 = 5).

Base: The term has different meanings in different areas of mathematics. It can mean a side of a triangle (geometry), repeated multiplication (exponential notation), the original number in percents (the "of" number), or the number of digits used in numerical or computer systems.

Coefficient: The number before a variable. In 3x, 3 is the coefficient.

Constant: A number or symbol that does not change, such as π, which is always 3.14….

Coordinate system: Two perpendicular number lines, called the x-axis and the y-axis, in a plane.

Coordinates: The two numbers that give the position of a point with respect to the axes in a coordinate system.

Customary system of measurement: The system based on pounds, ounces, yards, feet, and inches; used mainly in the US and some other English-speaking countries.

Denominator: The bottom number in a fraction. In $\frac{3}{5}$, 5 is the denominator.

Digits: The symbols used to write numbers. In the decimal system there are 10 digits: 0, 1, 2, 3, 4, 5, 6, 7, 8, and 9.

Dividend: The number to be divided. In long division, the dividend is inside the box. In 6 ÷ 3, 6 is the dividend.

Divisor: The number to divide by. In long division, the divisor is outside the box. In 6 ÷ 3, 3 is the divisor.

English system of measurement: See Customary system of measurement.

Estimation: An educated guess of the final answer to a calculation.

Evaluate: To find a numerical answer to a numerical expression or to an algebraic expression when the letters are exchanged for numbers.

Exponent: A number written as a superscript that tells how many equal factors a number has.
In $2^3 = 2 \times 2 \times 2$, 3 is the exponent and 2 is the factor. You can also say that 2 is raised to the power of 3.

Factor: A number that divides exactly into another number. For example, 12 has six factors: 1, 2, 3, 4, 6, and 12.

FOIL: An acronym for a method of multiplying two sums or differences (binomials). FOIL stand for "first, outer, inner, last."

Fractions: Numbers that are written as a division between two numbers, positive or negative. The top number (numerator) of a fraction can be zero, but the bottom number (denominator) cannot. (Division by zero is undefined.)

Function: A rule that turns a number (the independent variable) into another number (the dependent variable). The rule is usually written as an equation of y (the dependent variable) as a function of x (the independent variable). In $y = 2x$, the rule is to double each x-number to obtain y.

Graph: A drawing to show the relationship of two numbers, often as functions.

Inequalities: A statement that two quantities ⟨
Symbols used with inequalities are: < (less
> (greater than), ≤ (less than or equal to), ⟩
or equal to), and ≠ (not equal to).

Integers: The positive integers are the same as the ⟩⟩⟩⟩g
numbers (1, 2, 3,...). Together with 0 and the negative
integers (−1, −2, −3,...), they form the set of integers.

Intercepts: The points where a line crosses the axes of a graph.

Inverse operations: Two operations that cancel each other out
(provided that you use the same numbers).
Addition and subtraction are inverse operations, as are
multiplication and division. For example, $2 + 3 - 3 = 2$ and
$4 \times 5 \div 5 = 4$.

Laws (Principles and Properties): See Appendix 3 on page 23.

Magnitude: The size of a number. The magnitude is also called
the absolute value.

Mean: Commonly called the average or arithmetic mean, this is
the total of all entries divided by the number of entries for
some data.

Median: A term used in statistics for the middle term of data.
6 is the median in the series 2, 4, 6, 7, 9.

Metric system: The system of measurement used in scientific
measurement that is based on powers of 10. It is widely
used in Europe and is becoming more common in the
United States.

Mode: The number (or numbers) that occurs most frequently
in a group of numbers. 3 is the mode in the series
1, 3, 5, 3, 6, 3, 8, 3.

Multiple: A number that is a product of a given integer and any
other integer. Multiples of 5 include 10, 15, and 20.

Number: The abstract concept of amount. Symbols for numbers
are called numerals. See also Appendix 1 on page 19.

Number line: A straight line to illustrate the relationship of numbers to each other.

Numerator: The top number in a fraction.

In $\frac{3}{5}$, 3 is the numerator.

Operation: The action of one number on another according to the operation symbols ($+,-,\times,\div$) involved. The basic operations are addition, subtraction, multiplication, and division.

Order of operations: The order in which arithmetical operations are to be done.

First simplify inside all grouping symbols (any kind of parentheses and also above and/or below a fraction bar). Next, evaluate all expressions that contain exponents or roots (square roots for example). Then multiply/divide from left to right. Addition and subtraction are done last in any order.

The following mnemonic phrase is often used for the order of operations: Please Excuse My Dear Aunt Sally (parentheses, exponents, multiplication, division, addition, subtraction).

Ordered pair: Two numbers that are written in a specified order such as first x, then y. Points on a graph are ordered pairs and written (3,5) or (x,y).

Percent: The word means "divide by 100." The percent numbers most often refer to "percent of." Many people remember percent problems as "is, of, percent, 100." For example: "What is 50% of 60?" can be written as $\frac{x}{60} = \frac{50}{100}$ and then solved by cross-multiplication.

Pi (π): A constant often used in geometrical calculations that cannot be expressed as a fraction or decimal. An approximation is 3.14. When the circumference of a circle is divided by its diameter, π is the quotient.

Place value: The value of the position in a number. In the decimal system all places have values of a power of 10. For example, in 20, 2 has the value of 2×10, but in 200, the value of 2 is $2 \times 100 = 2 \times 10^2$.

Power: The word indicates repeated multiplication. The 4th power of 3 is written as 3^4, where 3 is the base and 4 the exponent.

Prefix: Letters placed before a word in order to change its meaning. Common prefixes for gram, meter, and liter in the metric system are kilo, hecto, deka, deci, centi, and milli.

Prime number: A number that can be divided only by 1 and the number itself. Some prime numbers are 2, 3, 5, 7, 11, and 13.

Proportion: Two fractions that are equal. An example of a proportion is $\frac{2}{5} = \frac{4}{10}$, whereby 2 is to 5 as 4 is to 10.

Ratio: A comparison of two numbers by division. For example, 2 is to 5 is written $\frac{2}{5}$ or $2 : 5$.

Reading numbers: A three-digit number such as 123 is read "one hundred twenty-three." A six-digit number such as 123,456 is read "one hundred twenty-three thousand four hundred fifty-six."
The decimal point is read as "and" or "point." The number 12.3 is "twelve and three tenths" or "twelve point three."

Root: The same as a solution to an equation. In the equation $x + 5 = 7$, 2 is a root. Root can also mean the opposite of raising to a power, such as the square root of 9 ($\sqrt{9}$) which is 3, because $3^2 = 9$.

Rounding: Approximating a number by replacing the last digit or digits with zeros in a whole number and dropping them in a decimal fraction. The numbers 4,985 and 5,008 could both be rounded to 5,000, and 0.49 could be 0.5.

Symbol: A letter or a sign that represents a concept or a word. The 10 symbols for numbers are called numerals, a plus sign ($+$) represents positive or addition, and x represents an unknown quantity.

Term: Numbers or variables that are separated by addition or subtraction.

Translations: See Appendix 2 on page 21.

Unit: A standard to express the quantity one. For example, the length of the meter is a unit for length measurements.

Variable: A letter that can represent any number.
In $y = 2x$, both x and y are variables; 2 is a constant.

1

NUMBERS

Real numbers are all numbers that can be found on a number line by counting, measuring, or geometric construction. They exist in the real world. There are many different kinds of numbers belonging to the real numbers.

Natural numbers:

The numbers shown on the following number line are called **natural** numbers. Another name for them is **counting** numbers or **positive integers**.

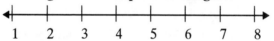

Whole numbers:

Natural numbers, together with 0.

Negative integers:

Numbers on the other side of 0.
Examples are –1, –2, –3, ...

Integers:

Natural numbers, the negative of these numbers, and 0.

Rational numbers:

Numbers that are ratios (division) of two integers.
Examples are: $\frac{4}{5}, \frac{2}{9}, \frac{4}{1}$.

Fractions as well as integers are rational numbers.
Decimal fractions are fractions with denominators of 10, 100, etc. ($\frac{1}{10}, \frac{1}{100}, \frac{1}{1000}$). All of these numbers can be found on a number line.

Irrational numbers:

There is still room on the number line for more numbers. Irrational numbers cannot be located by usual means because they cannot be expressed as rational numbers. An example of an irrational number is $\sqrt{2}$, which can be found on the number line by construction of a right triangle with legs equal to 1.

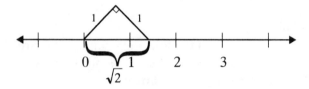

The hypotenuse is $\sqrt{2}$. An *approximate* value for $\sqrt{2}$ is 1.414. π is also an irrational number. It is the quotient between the circumference of a circle and the diameter and is *approximately* 3.14.

Imaginary numbers: If a number is not real (that is, neither a rational nor an irrational number), it is **imaginary**. An example is the square root of –4.

2

Translations

Addition

Terms (or addends) are added to give the sum. The order of the terms does not matter.

The following phrases are all translated into $a + b$:

- the sum of a and b
- a plus b
- a increased by b
- b more than a
- add b to a

Subtraction

One term is subtracted from another to give the difference. The order of the terms *is* important, because $5 - 2$ is *not* equal to $2 - 5$.

In a translation the "from" number comes first and the "less than" comes last.

Subtract 3 from 7 is $7 - 3$ and 5 less than 9 is $9 - 5$

The following phrases are all translated as $a - b$:

- the difference of a and b
- a minus b
- a decreased by b
- b subtracted from a
- a less b
- b less than a
- take away b from a

Multiplication

Two factors (sometimes called multiplier and multiplicand) multiplied together give the product. The order of the factors does not matter.

The following phrases are all translated as ab or $a \times b$ or $a(b)$:

- ◆ the product of a and b
- ◆ a times b
- ◆ a multiplied by b

Division

The dividend is divided by the divisor to produce the quotient. The order is important, because $6 \div 3 = 2$ but $3 \div 6 = 0.5$.

The following phrases can all be translated as $a \div b$ or a/b or $\frac{a}{b}$:

- ◆ the quotient of a and b
- ◆ a divided by b
- ◆ b goes into a

Equal

The following phrases are all translated into an equal sign ($=$):

- ◆ is, is equal to
- ◆ equals
- ◆ is the same as
- ◆ the result is

The phrase "not equal to" is written in symbols as $\neq$.

Inequalities

With numbers we always know which number is greater or smaller and use the symbols $<$ for smaller than and $>$ for greater than. In algebra, we sometimes need symbols for "less than or equal to" and "greater than or equal to."

- ◆ a is greater than b $a > b$
- ◆ a is greater than or equal to b $a \geq b$
- ◆ a is less than b $a < b$
- ◆ a is less than or equal to b $a \leq b$

3

Properties

The Commutative Property

In addition and multiplication the order can be reversed:

$5 + 2 = 7$ and $2 + 5 = 7$
$5(2) = 10$ and $2(5) = 10$

This is the commutative property. In variables it is stated

$a + b = b + a$
$a(b) = b(a)$

This property does *not* hold for subtraction and division.

$5 - 2 = 3$ but $2 - 5 = -3$
$4 \div 2 = 2$ but $2 \div 4 = 0.5$

The Associative Property

In addition and multiplication of three numbers, it doesn't matter whether you combine the first two numbers and then the third, or if you start by combining the second and third numbers and then the first.

$(3 + 7) + 4 = 10 + 4 = 14$ and
$3 + (7 + 4) = 3 + 11 = 14$

$(3 \cdot 7) 4 = 21 \cdot 4 = 84$ and
$3(7 \cdot 4) = 3 \cdot 28 = 84$

In variables the associative law states:

$(a + b) + c = a + (b + c)$
$(ab)c = a(bc)$

Subtraction and division are *not* associative.

$$(5 - 2) - 3 = 3 - 3 = 0 \quad \text{but}$$
$$5 - (2 - 3) = 5 - (-1) = 5 + 1 = 6$$

$$(4 \div 2) \div 2 = 2 \div 2 = 1 \text{ but}$$
$$4 \div (2 \div 2) = 4 \div 1 = 4$$

The Distributive Property

Multiplication can be distributed over addition or subtraction.

$$4(2 + 3) = 4(5) = 20 \text{ and}$$
$$4(2) + 4(3) = 8 + 12 = 20$$

In variables:

$$a(b + c) = ab + ac$$

Division cannot be distributed over addition or subtraction.

$$10 \div (2 + 3) = \frac{10}{2+3} = \frac{10}{5} = 2 \quad \text{but}$$

$$10 \div 2 + 10 \div 3 = \frac{10}{2} + \frac{10}{3} = 5 + 3\frac{1}{3} = 8\frac{1}{3}$$

In variables:

$$\frac{a}{(b+c)} \neq \frac{a}{b} + \frac{a}{c}$$

ABSCISSA

Definition: The *x*-COORDINATE of a point on a graph. It is the horizontal distance from the *y*-axis to a certain point as well as the first number in an ORDERED PAIR.

See also GRAPHING.

Example: In (4,3), 4 is the abscissa.

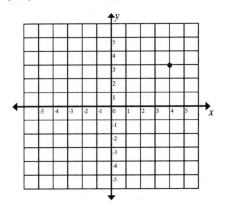

Practice: Find the abscissa:

a) in the graph

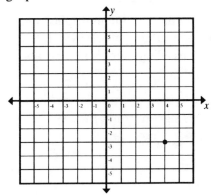

b) in the ordered pair (3,4)

ABSOLUTE VALUE

Definition: The magnitude (size) of a number. It is always positive. It can be represented by the distance between zero and a number on the NUMBER LINE.

In calculations, drop the positive or negative sign and replace the absolute value symbol, consisting of two vertical lines, with parentheses.

Symbol: | |

Examples:

1) Number line

2) $|+2| = 2$

3) $|-2| = 2$

4) $|-1| + |3| = (1) + (3) = 4$
   Keep the + sign between the absolute values. It means addition.

5) $|2||-4| = (2)(4) = 8$
   There is an understood multiplication sign between the absolute value symbols as well as between the parentheses when there is no operation symbol between them.

6) $-|-5| = -(5) = -5$
   The minus sign in front of the symbol | | is kept.

Practice: Find the value of

   a) $|-3| + |-6| - |1|$

   b) $|-1| |7|$

   c) $2|-2|$

Acute Angle

Definition: An ANGLE that measures between $0°$ and $90°$.

Examples:

1)

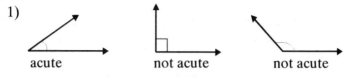

acute   not acute   not acute

2) A 15-degree angle is acute.

Addends

Definition: The numbers that are added. These numbers are also called TERMS.

Examples:

1) In $1 + 2 = 3$, 1 and 2 are addends and 3 is the SUM.

2) In $2 + 4 + 9$, 2, 4, and 9 are addends.

Addition

Definition: To combine TERMS (addends) into one SUM. See also TRANSLATIONS (in Appendix 2 on page 21).

Symbol: +

Examples:

1) The sum of 2 and 3 is 5.

2) 3 added to 2 is 5.

3) $2 + 3 = 5$

Addition Method (for solving equations)

Definition: A method of solving SIMULTANEOUS EQUATIONS, which means two or more equations with two or more unknowns (variables). The equations are combined by addition to eliminate one variable.

The COEFFICIENTS of one of the variables must be the same but with opposite signs. If the coefficients are not the same, one (or both) of the equations must be multiplied by a suitable number to make the coefficients equal and with opposite signs.

Examples:

1) $5x + 2y = 9$
$3x - 2y = -1$
$\overline{8x \qquad = 8}$ The equations are added.

$\dfrac{8x}{8} \quad = \dfrac{8}{8}$ Divide both sides by 8.

$x = 1$

Replace x with 1 in the first (or second) equation to determine y.

$5(1) + 2y = 9$
$2y = 4$
$y = 2$

Answer: $x = 1$ and $y = 2$
$3(1) - 2(2) = 3 - 4 = -1$ The solution is correct.

2) $x + y = 7$
$-x + y = 1$
$\overline{2y = 8}$
$y = 4$
$x + 4 = 7$
$x = 3$

Answer: $x = 3$ and $y = 4$

3) $2x + 3y = 7$
$3x - 2y = 4$

To make the coefficients of the y variable the same, multiply the first equation with 2 and the second with 3:

$4x + 6y = 14$
$9x - 6y = 12$ Add the equations:
$\overline{13x = 26}$
$x = 2$

Replace x in the first equation with 2:

$2(2) + 3y = 7$

$3y = 3$

$y = 1$

Practice:

Solve and check your solutions:

a) $3x - 4y = 4$

$x + 4y = 12$

b) $-5x + 2y = 1$

$5x + 5y = 20$

c) $4x + 5y = 37$

$2x + y = 11$ Hint: Multiply this equation with a negative number!

ADDITIVE IDENTITY ELEMENT

Definition: A number that, when added to any number, does not change the value of the number. 0 is the additive identity element.

Example:

$5 + 0 = 5$

ADJACENT ANGLES

Definition: ANGLES that have a common side between them.

Example:

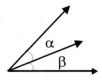

α and β are adjacent angles.

Age Problems

Definition: Problems that deal with people's ages.

Template (form):

Name	Current Age	Age in n years
	A	$A + n$
	B	$B + n$

Example:

Fritz is five years younger than Maryanne. In three years she will be twice his age then. How old is Fritz now?

To solve, assume that Maryanne is x years old. Fritz is $x - 5$ years old, then, because he is five year younger.

	Current Age	Age in 3 years
Maryanne	x	$x + 3$
Fritz	$x - 5$	$x - 5 + 3$
		(which equals $x - 2$)

Equation: $x + 3 = 2(x - 2)$

$x + 3 = 2x - 4$

$7 = x$

Answer: Maryanne is 7 years old and
Fritz is $7 - 5 = 2$ years old.

Practice:

1) Solve the example above by assuming that Fritz is x years old and Maryanne is $x + 5$ years old.

2) Brita is 30 years older than her daughter Eva. Ten years ago, the mother was twice as old as her daughter was then. How old is Eva now?

Algebra

Definition: Arithmetic that is generalized to include variable terms. This branch of mathematics uses symbols (letters) called VARIABLES to represent numbers.

Examples:

1) $2a + 3a = 5a$, where a can mean any number.

2) $x + 5 = 9$, where x represents the number 4.

Algebraic Equation

Definition: An EQUATION containing one or more VARIABLES.

Examples:

1) $x + 5 = 9$
2) $x^2 + 3x + 2 = 0$
3) $x + y = 5$

Algebraic Expression

Definition: One or more TERMS containing VARIABLES and CONSTANTS. Note that a given expression does not contain an equal sign.

Examples:

1) $3x^2 + 4x - 5$
2) $x - 2y + 5z + 7$

Algorithm

Definition: A series of steps that must be followed in order to solve certain problems. The algorithm tells exactly what to do first, second, and so on.

Examples:

1) The steps used to perform a long division problem.

2) A FLOWCHART (that is, a chart showing the steps from starting material to product).

3) Computer programs, which are step-by-step instructions written in a language such as BASIC or LOGO.

ALTERNATE ANGLES

Definition: Angles formed by a line intersecting two given lines.

Examples:

1)

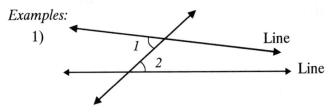

Angles *1* and *2* are alternate *interior* angles.

2)

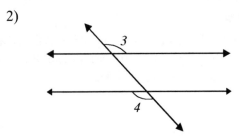

Angles *3* and *4* are alternate *exterior* angles.

Practice:

Mark all sets of two alternate (interior and exterior) angles in the figure: Use one letter or number for each different pair of angles.

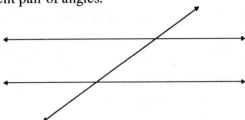

ALTITUDE

Definition: The PERPENDICULAR distance from the BASE of a figure to the opposite VERTEX. The altitude is also called the height. A triangle has three altitudes. Any side can be considered the base.

Examples: *h* is the altitude.

1)

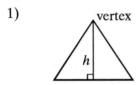

2)

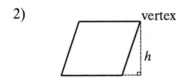

Practice: Draw the altitude to the side marked *b*.

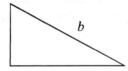

ANGLE

Definition: Two RAYS (half lines) or straight lines coming together at a point, called a VERTEX, form an angle. An angle is measured in degrees.

Examples:

1)

2)

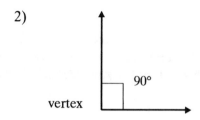

APPROXIMATION

Definition: You make an approximation when you ROUND a number to one or two whole number DIGITS to make the calculation easier. See also ESTIMATION.

Symbol: ≈

Examples:

1) $453 + 687 \approx 500 + 700 \approx 1200$

2) $3694 \div 69 \approx 4000 \div 70 \approx 60$

Practice:

Approximate the sum of 1,863 and 4,828. Use first only one non-zero digit and then two non-zero digits to convince yourself that the answers are (approximately) the same. Check the correct answer with a calculator.

ARC

Definition: Part of the CIRCUMFERENCE of a circle.

Example:

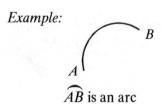

$\overset{\frown}{AB}$ is an arc

Symbol: ⌒

34

AREA

Definition: The amount of surface inside a plane figure. Area is measured in square units.

Formulas:

RECTANGLE: Area $A = lw$,
where l = length
and w = width.

SQUARE: Area $A = s^2$,
where s = side.

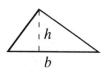

TRIANGLE: Area $A = \frac{1}{2}bh$,
where b = base and
h = height (altitude).

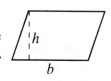

PARALLELOGRAM: Area $A = bh$,
where b = base
and h = height.

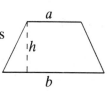

TRAPEZOID: Area $A = \frac{1}{2}(a + b)h$,
where a and b are bases
and h = height.

CIRCLE: Area $A = \pi r^2$,
where r is the radius.

Examples:

1) The area of a rectangle with a length of 5 cm and a width of 2 cm is 5 cm $\times$ 2 cm = 10 cm^2.

2) The area of a square with a side of 3 inches is 9 square inches.

3) The area of a triangle with a base of 4 cm and a height of 3 cm is $\frac{1}{2}$(4 cm)(3 cm) = 6 cm^2.

4) The area of a parallelogram with a base of 5 cm and a height of 4 cm is 5 cm $\times$ 4 cm = 20 cm^2.

5) The area of a trapezoid with sides 4 inches and 6 inches and with a height of 3 inches is $\frac{1}{2}$(4 inches + 6 inches)(3 inches) = 15 square inches.

6) The area of a circle with radius 5 cm is $\pi 5^2$ cm^2 = 25π cm^2 $\approx$ 78.5 cm^2. ($\pi \approx 3.14$)

Practice:

Find the area of the following figure, which consists of one square and one semicircle (half-circle). The side of the square as well as the diameter of the semicircle (two times the radius) is 1 inch.

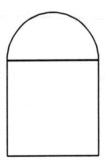

ARITHMETIC

Definition: The branch of mathematics concerned with operations (addition, subtraction, etc.) on numbers and the properties of numbers. See also TRANSLATIONS (in Appendix 2 on page 21).

ARITHMETIC MEAN

See MEAN.

ASSOCIATIVE LAW

Definition: When you add (or multiply) three numbers, you can add (or multiply) the first two numbers and then the third number, or you can first add (or multiply) the second and third numbers and then the first number.

Formulas:
$$(a + b) + c = a + (b + c)$$
$$(ab)c = a(bc)$$

Examples:

1) $1 + 2 + 3 = $
$$(1 + 2) + 3 = 3 + 3 = 6$$
$$\text{or}$$
$$1 + (2 + 3) = 1 + 5 = 6$$

2) $2 \times 3 \times 4 = $
$$(2 \times 3) \times 4 = 6 \times 4 = 24$$
$$\text{or}$$
$$2 \times (3 \times 4) = 2 \times 12 = 24$$

Practice:

Use the associative law to calculate the following examples two ways:

a) $25 + 13 + 12$

b) $(3)(2)(5)$

AVERAGE

Definition: The sum of the items divided by the number of items. Also called the arithmetic mean or simply the MEAN. Statistics deals with three types of averages: MEAN, MEDIAN, and MODE.

Examples:

1) The average of 6, 9, 4, and 5 is
$$\frac{6 + 9 + 4 + 5}{4} = \frac{24}{4} = 6$$

2) A total of $1,431 was collected from nine contributors. What was the average contribution? $1,431 \div 9 = 159$. The average contribution was $159.

Practice:

a) Find the average of 1, 2, 2, 4, and 6.

b) The farmer collected 90 liters of milk from five cows. How much milk did he get from each cow on the average?

AXIS (AXES)

In coordinate systems:

Definition: The horizontal ( ) and the vertical (|) line in a COORDINATE SYSTEM The plural form of axis is <u>axes</u>.

Example:

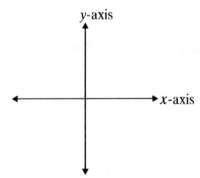

In symmetry:

Definition: An axis is a line that divides a figure into two matching parts. They are called congruent (equal in both shape and size) parts.

Examples:

1)

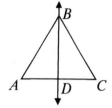

     Line *BD* is an axis of symmetry in the triangle *ABC*. Triangles *ABD* and *CBD* are congruent triangles.

2) The diagonal is an axis of symmetry in a square:

Practice:

    Find all axes of symmetry in the square above.

BAR GRAPH

Definition: A graph consisting of bars showing quantities in a set of data.

Example:

The following graph depicts the numbers of M&Ms in a small package:

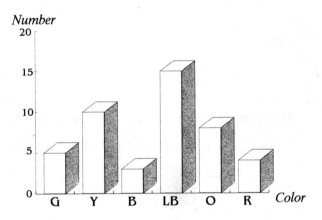

Practice:

How many yellow M&Ms are there in this package?

BASE

In percents:

Definition: The whole or the original number. (Sometimes it is referred to as the "of" number.) See also PERCENT.

Examples:

1) In 5% of 10, 10 is the base.

2) In "25% of what number is 40?" "what number" is the base.

$$40 \div 0.25 = 160 \quad \text{The base is 160.}$$

3) The price was $210 after 5% tax was added.
   What was the price without tax?
   $210 \div 1.05 = 200$
   The base (original price) was $200.
   (5% of 200 is 10; 200 + 10 = 210)

Practice:

Find the base:

a) 6% of 30 is 18

b) 5 is what percent of 20?

c) Macy's had a sale where I got 20% off. I paid $40 for my purchases. How much did they cost originally?

In geometry:

Definition: The side of a figure to which the ALTITUDE is drawn from the VERTEX and PERPENDICULAR to the side. The base is often at the bottom of a figure but does not have to be.

Example:

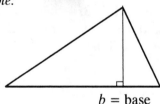

$b =$ base

Practice:

If a is the altitude, where is the base b?

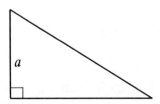

In exponential notation:

Definition: The base is the number that is multiplied by itself several times. It is called the FACTOR.

Examples:

1) In 2^5, 2 is the base. $2^5 = 2 \times 2 \times 2 \times 2 \times 2 = 32$

2) In $(-5)^2 = (-5)(-5) = 25$, -5 is the base.

3) In $-3^2 = -(3)(3) = -9$, 3 is the base.

4) In a^b, a is the base.

Practice:

Find the base:

a) 5^2

b) $-(-7)^3$

c) x^y

In numeration systems:

Definition: The number of DIGITS used. There are 10 digits in the base 10, decimal system (0, 1, 2, 3, 4, 5, 6, 7, 8, and 9). There are 2 digits (0 and 1) in the base two (or BINARY) system, which is used in computer programs.

Examples:

1) Base five uses the digits 0, 1, 2, 3, and 4.

2) Base 16 uses the symbols A, B, C, D, E, and F to supplement our 10-digit system (0, 1, 2, 3, ..., 9, A, B, C, D, E, F).

Practice:

List the digits in the octal (base eight) system.

BASIC OPERATIONS

Definition: Addition, subtraction, multiplication, and division are called the basic operations. See also TRANSLATIONS in Appendix 2 on page 21.

Examples:

1) Add 4 to 6:   6 + 4
2) Subtract 5 from 9: 9 − 5
3) Multiply 7 by 8:   7 × 8
4) Divide 81 by 3:   81 ÷ 3

BINARY

In numeration systems:

Definition: A system that has only two digits: 0 and 1. It is used in computers because they can be programmed to respond to an on-off state. It is also called the base two system.

Decimal system:	Binary system:
1	1
2	10
3	11
4	100
5	101
6	110
7	111
8	1000
9	1001
10	1010
11	1011
12	1100

When we add nine and one in our normal (the decimal) system, there is no single symbol for the sum. Instead we have to regroup and call the answer 10. This is, of course, pronounced "ten." Similarly, in the base two system, we have no symbols for numbers larger than 1 and have to regroup more often. The numbers we can use are 0, 1, 10, 11, 100, 101, 110, 111, 1000, and so on. These numbers are like our decimal system based on PLACE VALUES. Instead of having places with values of 1, 10, 100, etc. (that is, powers of 10), we have places with powers of 2 (that is, 1, 2, 4, 8, 16, 32, etc.).

The number 10 (base 2) is pronounced "one, zero" and can also be written 10_{two}.

What is 10 (base 2) in the decimal system? "1" is in the place worth 2 and 0 in the place worth 1. Therefore, the number is $1 \times 2 + 0 \times 1 = 2$.

Examples:

1) In the binary system, add 101 and 111:

$$\overset{1\ 1}{101}$$
$$+111$$
$$\overline{1100} \quad \textit{Regroup}$$

$1 + 1 = 10_{two}$
$1 + 0 + 1 = 10_{two}$
$1 + 1 + 1 = 11_{two}$

2) In decimal notation *Example* 1) would be:

(Use PLACE VALUES)

$$101 = \quad 4 + 0 + 1 = 5$$
$$+111 = \quad 4 + 2 + 1 = \underline{7}$$
$$1100 = 8 + 4 + 0 + 0 = 12$$

Practice:

a) Add the binary numbers $1011 + 1110$.

b) Write the decimal number 6 in the binary system.

In operations:

Definition: An operation that combines two numbers to give a third.

Examples:

1) Addition, subtraction, and multiplication are binary operations.

2) To take the square root of a number is <u>not</u> a binary operation.

BINOMIAL

Definition: An expression made up of two TERMS.

Examples:

1) $a + b$

2) $3ax - 5$

BISECTOR

Definition: A point or a line that cuts a figure into two matching (CONGRUENT) parts.

Examples:

1)

Point C bisects the line segment $\overline{AB}$.

2)

$\overrightarrow{AD}$ bisects the angle *BAC*.

CARTESIAN COORDINATE SYSTEM

Definition: Two perpendicular NUMBER LINES, called the x-axis and the y-axis create four equal parts in a plane. These are called quadrants. Quadrant I is in the northeast corner of the graph. Quadrant II in the northwest, Quadrant III in southwest and Quadrant IV in southeast.

Any point in the plane is identified by two numbers, the x- and y-COORDINATES. The x-coordinate refers to the horizontal (x-) axis and the y-coordinate to the vertical (y-) axis. The point at which the number lines cross is called the origin. See also GRAPH.

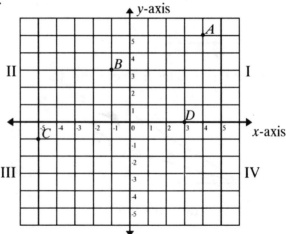

Example:

Both x- and y-coordinates are positive in Quadrant I: the coordinates of the point A are $x = +4, y = +5$. x is negative and y is positive in Quadrant II: the coordinates of point B are $x = -1, y = +3$.

Practice:

In which quadrant are both coordinates negative? What are the coordinates of points C and D?

CELSIUS

Definition: The international unit of temperature formerly known as centigrade. (1 degree Celsius = 1.8 degrees Fahrenheit) See also TEMPERATURE.

Symbol: $^{\circ}C$

Examples:

1) Water freezes at $0^{\circ}C$ $(32^{\circ}F)$.

2) Water boils at $100^{\circ}C$ $(212^{\circ}F)$.

CENTI-

Definition: A Latin PREFIX standing for 0.01 (that is, one hundredth). See also METRIC SYSTEM.

Examples:

1) One centimeter equals 0.01 meter;
   1 meter equals 100 centimeters.

2) One centiliter equals 0.01 liter;
   1 liter = 100 centiliters.

Practice:

How many centigrams are there in one gram?

CENTRAL ANGLE

Definition: An angle in a circle with the VERTEX at the center of the CIRCLE.

Example:

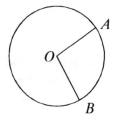

$\angle AOB$ is a central angle.
O is the center of the circle.

Practice:

Name the central angle in the following:

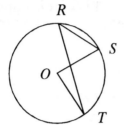

CHORD

Definition: A LINE SEGMENT (part of a straight line) that joins two points on a curve.

Example:

1)

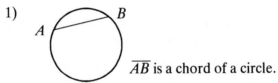

$\overline{AB}$ is a chord of a circle.

2)

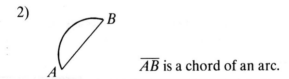

$\overline{AB}$ is a chord of an arc.

Practice:

Can a chord go through the center of the circle?

CIRCLE

Definition: A CLOSED CURVE consisting of all the points that are at a fixed distance (the radius *r*) from a certain point (the center).

To draw a circle, use either a compass or a piece of string with a pencil connected to one end and a thumbtack to the other. Fasten the thumbtack on a piece of paper and trace a curve with the pencil while keeping the string stretched. The length of the string is the radius, the position of the thumbtack the center, and the curve the circle.

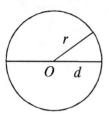

Point O is the center.

The diameter (d) equals twice the radius (r); $d = 2r$.

The circumference (the length of the curve) of a circle equals $2\pi r$ (or πd), where $\pi \approx 3.14$ or $\frac{22}{7}$. 3.14 and $\frac{22}{7}$ are approximations of the number π (PI).

The area of a circle equals πr^2.

Examples:

1) The circumference of a circle with a radius of 2 cm is $2\pi(2) \approx 2 \times 3.14 \times 2 = 12.56$ cm. The circumference is approximately 12.56.

2) The area of a circle with a radius of 2 cm is $\pi(2)^2 \approx 3.14 \times 4 = 12.56$ square centimeters (cm²). The area is approximately 12.56 cm².

3) The circumference of a circle with a radius of $\frac{7}{11}$ cm is $\approx 2\left(\frac{22}{7}\right)\left(\frac{7}{11}\right) = 2(2) = 4$ cm.

4) The area of a circle with a diameter of 10 cm is $\pi\left(\frac{10}{2}\right)^2 = \pi 5^2 = 25\pi \approx 78.5$ cm².

49

Practice:

Find the circumference and area of a circle with a radius of 4 inches.

CIRCLE GRAPH

Definition: A circle that shows data expressed as percents as sectors (like slices of pie). It is similar to a BAR GRAPH, which is horizontal. (The circle (pie) graph is circular.)

100% is expressed as 360° (the whole circle), 50% is 180°, and so on. It is convenient to use a PROTRACTOR in the construction of this type of graph. To use the protractor, first draw a radius. Place the 0-180 line of the protractor on the radius with the protractor center on the circle center. Make a point at the desired number of degrees. Connect this point with the circle center. Use this new radius as the 0-180 line and proceed as before.

Example:

Make a pie graph showing the following information: 25 M&M candies are in a bowl. There are 5 green, 5 yellow, 2 red, 3 dark brown, and 10 light brown.

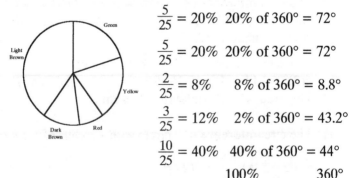

$$\frac{5}{25} = 20\% \quad 20\% \text{ of } 360° = 72°$$

$$\frac{5}{25} = 20\% \quad 20\% \text{ of } 360° = 72°$$

$$\frac{2}{25} = 8\% \quad 8\% \text{ of } 360° = 8.8°$$

$$\frac{3}{25} = 12\% \quad 2\% \text{ of } 360° = 43.2°$$

$$\frac{10}{25} = 40\% \quad 40\% \text{ of } 360° = 44°$$

$$100\% \qquad 360°$$

Practice:

Make a pie graph showing 50%, 25%, 15% and 10%.

CIRCUMFERENCE

Definition: The length of the line making up a circle. It is $2\pi r$, where r is the radius of the circle and π is the number PI, which is approximately 3.14 (≈ 3.14).

Example:

The circumference of a circle with a radius of 1 inch is $2(3.14)1 = 6.28$ inches.

Practice:

Find the circumference of a circle that has a radius of 4 centimeters.

CIRCUMSCRIBED FIGURE

Definition: A geometric figure that is drawn exactly around another geometric figure. The figures involved are usually one circle and one POLYGON, such as a triangle or a square. Compare with INSCRIBED.

Examples:

1) The square is circumscribed around (or about) the circle.

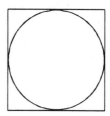

2) The circle passes through all VERTICES (corners) of the triangle, which is circumscribed by the circle.

CLOSED CURVE

Definition: A curve that starts at a point and comes back to that point.

Examples:

1)

2)

COEFFICIENT

Definition: The number before a VARIABLE (such as x, y, etc.). It is the same as the NUMERICAL COEFFICIENT.

Example:

1) In $5x$, 5 is the coefficient.

2) In $-x^2$, -1 is the coefficient.

Practice:

Find the coefficient in $-4xyz$.

COLLINEAR

Definition: Points lying on the same line.

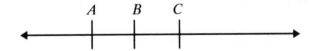

Examples:

1) The points (1,2), (2,1), and (−1,4) are collinear in the graph below. They all satisfy the equation $x + y = 3$ ($1 + 2 = 3, 2 + 1 = 3$, and $−1 + 4 = 3$), which is a graph of a straight line. See also GRAPH.

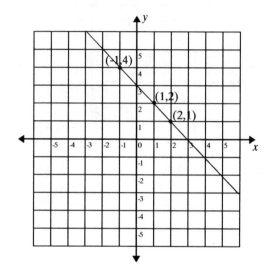

2) The points (2,7), (0,3), and (−2,−1) are collinear in the graph on the following page. The SLOPES (steepness or "rise over run") of the lines between any two pairs of points are the same. The slope is usually notated with the letter m.

$$m_1 = \frac{7-3}{2-0} = \frac{4}{2} = 2$$

$$m_2 = \frac{3-(-1)}{0-(-2)} = \frac{4}{2} = 2$$

$$m_3 = \frac{7-(-1)}{2-(-2)} = \frac{8}{4} = 2$$

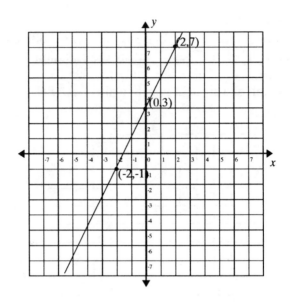

Practice:

Are the points (2,7), (0,3) and (−1, −2) collinear?

COMBINING LIKE TERMS

Definition: To add or subtract terms that are like (that is, have exactly the same letters and exponents).

Examples:

1) Combine the x- terms: $5x + 3x = 8x$.

2) Combine the matching terms:
$3a^2b - 4ab^2 + 2a^2b = 5a^2b - 4ab^2$

Practice:

Add all like terms in the following:
$4xy^2 + 3xy + 5xy + xy^2$

Common Denominator

Definition: A DENOMINATOR that is the same for two or more FRACTIONS. It has to be divisible by all denominators of the various fractions. Fractions with common denominators are called like fractions.
See also LEAST COMMON DENOMINATOR (LCD).

Examples:

1) $\frac{1}{5}$ and $\frac{3}{5}$ have 5 as a common denominator.

2) $\frac{1}{3}$ and $\frac{5}{6}$ have 6 as a common denominator, because $\frac{1}{3}$ can be written as $\frac{2}{6}$. 12, 18, and 24 are also common denominators, because $\frac{1}{3}$ can be written as $\frac{4}{12}$ or $\frac{6}{18}$ or $\frac{8}{24}$, and $\frac{5}{6}$ can be written as $\frac{10}{12}$ or $\frac{15}{18}$ or $\frac{20}{24}$.

Practice:

Which of the following are common denominators to $\frac{1}{2}, \frac{4}{5}$, and $\frac{3}{10}$: 5, 10, 15, 20, 25, 30?

Common Factor

Definition: A WHOLE NUMBER that divides exactly two or more numbers. See also GREATEST COMMON FACTOR.

Examples:

1) 16 and 24 have 2, 4, and 8 as common factors. In other words, 16 and 24 can both be divided by 2, 4, and 8.

2   $3a^2$ and $9a$ have 3, a, and $3a$ as common factors. In other words, $3a^2$ and $9a$ can be divided by 3, a and $3a$.

Practice:

List the common factors of 15 and 30.

Common Fractions

See FRACTIONS.

Common Multiple

Definition: A WHOLE NUMBER that is a MULTIPLE of each of some given numbers.

See also LEAST COMMON MULTIPLE (LCM).

Examples:

The multiples of 2 are 2, 4, 6, 8, 10, 12, 14, 16, 18, ...
The multiples of 3 are 3, 6, 9, 12, 15, 18, ...
6, 12, and 18, ... are multiples of both 2 and 3.
Therefore 6, 12, and 18 are common multiples.

Practice:

Find the first three common multiples of 6 and 9.

Commutative Operations

Definition: Operations in which the order of doing the operations does not matter. Addition and multiplication are commutative operations. Subtraction and division are not commutative operations.

Examples:

1) $a + b = b + a$ (addition)
   $2 + 3 = 5$
   $3 + 2 = 5$

2) $a(b) = b(a)$ (multiplication)
   $2(5) = 10$
   $5(2) = 10$

3) $2 - 3 = -1$ (subtraction)
   $3 - 2 = 1$

4) $4 \div 2 = 2$ (division)
   $2 \div 4 = 0.5$

COMPLEMENTARY ANGLES

Definition: Two angles whose measure adds up to 90°.

Examples:

1) $20°$ and $70°$ $(20 + 70 = 90)$

2)

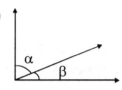

α and β are complementary angles.

COMPLETING THE SQUARE

Definition: A method of adding a number to an expression in order to get a TRINOMIAL that can be rewritten as a PERFECT SQUARE. For example, if 4 is added to the expression $x^2 + 4x$, we get $x^2 + 4x + 4 = (x + 2)^2$ by using the following formula. Check that this is correct by multiplying.

$(x + 2)(x + 2) = x^2 + 2x + 2x + 4 = x^2 + 4x + 4$

Formula: $x^2 + 2ax + a^2 = (x + a)^2$ or
        $x^2 - 2ax + a^2 = (x - a)^2$

This formula can be derived the following way by factoring:

$$x^2 + 2ax + a^2 = x^2 + ax + ax + a^2$$
$$= x(x + a) + a(x + a)$$
$$= (x + a)(x + a) = (x + a)^2$$

Note that the operation symbol preceding the number to be added is always **positive**!

The number that is added is called the CONSTANT TERM. It should be the square of one-half of the COEFFICIENT of the x-term provided the coefficient of the x^2 term is 1. In the formula the coefficient of x is $2a$ and half of that is a. The square of a is a^2. See QUADRATIC EQUATIONS for cases when the coefficient of the x^2-term is different from 1.

Examples:

1) $x^2 + 6x + 9 = x^2 + 6x + 3^2 = (x + 3)^2$

2) $x^2 - 6x + 9 = x^2 - 6x + 3^2 = (x - 3)^2$

3) $x^2 - 5x + (\frac{5}{2})^2 = (x - \frac{5}{2})^2$

Practice:

What constant terms should be added to the following expressions, so that the trinomials are perfect squares?

a) $x^2 + 8x$

b) $x^2 - 8x + 2$

COMPLEX FRACTIONS

Definition: A fraction in which either the NUMERATOR or the DENOMINATOR is itself a fraction. See also FRACTIONS. A complex fraction can be rewritten as a division and simplified.

Examples:

1) $\dfrac{\frac{1}{3}}{4} = \frac{1}{3} \div 4 = \frac{1}{3} \times \frac{1}{4} = \frac{1}{12}$ (Division is changed to multiplication of the inverse.

Remember: $2 \div 4 = 2 \times \frac{1}{4} = \frac{2}{4} = \frac{1}{2}$)

2) $\dfrac{\frac{2}{3}}{\frac{4}{5}} = \frac{2}{3} \div \frac{4}{5} = \frac{2}{3} \times \frac{5}{4} = \frac{10}{12} = \frac{5}{6}$

Practice:

Rewrite $\dfrac{5}{\frac{11}{15}}$ as a simple fraction.

Composite Number

Definition: A WHOLE NUMBER that can be written as a multiplication (that is, FACTORED).
See also PRIME NUMBER.

Examples:

1) $6 = 2 \times 3$
   (2 and 3 are prime numbers and cannot be factored)

2) $16 = 4 \times 4$ or 2×8

Compound Interest

Definition: INTEREST paid not only on the PRINCIPAL (the money that is invested or borrowed) but also on the interest that is already added to the principal at certain times.

Formula: $A = P(1 + r)^t$, where A is the accumulated principal (that is, principal P plus interest), r is the RATE per COMPOUNDING PERIOD, and t is the number of times the interest is compounded (that is, calculated and added to the principal). The interest I is the difference between the accumulated principal and the principal.

Formula: $I = A - P$

Examples:

1) Find the accumulated principal after one year if \$200 is invested at a yearly rate of 4% and the interest is compounded monthly.
   $P = \$200$
   $r = 4\%/12 = 0.04/12 = 0.00333$
   $t = 12$
   $A = \$200(1 + 0.00333)^{12} = \$208.14$

Use a calculator for these calculations. The commas signify new keystrokes. Some calculators accept the input: 200 , x , (, 1+0.00333,) , y^x, 12 , =.
It is safer to do it the following way:
1+0.00333 , = , y^x, 12 , = , x , 200 , =.
Some calculators do not have the y^x, but have x^y which works the same way. Calculator answers might vary.

2) Find the interest on $1,000 invested for five years at a yearly rate of 6% compounded daily.
P = $1,000
r = 0.06/365 = 0.0001644
t = 365 × 5 = 1825
A = $1,000(1 + 0.0001644)^{1825}$ = $1349.87
I = $1349.87 – 1000 = $349.87
Answer: $349.87

Practice:

Find the interest on $200 invested at a yearly rate of 4% for 20 years. The interest is compounded
a) Monthly.

b) Yearly.

COMPOUNDING PERIOD

Definition: A certain length of time, such as one day or one month, after which INTEREST is COMPOUNDED (added to the PRINCIPAL).

Examples:

1) If the interest is compounded each month, the compounding period is 1 month or 1/12 year.

2) If the interest is compounded every day, the compounding period is 1 day or 1/365 year.

Concave

Definition: The word means curved inwards. A POLYGON is concave if at least one line segment (*AC*) connecting two points lies outside the figure. (See also CONVEX.)

Examples:

1)

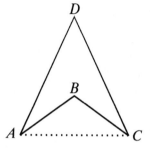

Note that the angle *inside* the polygon (*ABC*) is more than 180°. The dotted line shows that two points of the polygon are connected outside the polygon.

2)

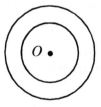

Concave mirror. The silvered side is inside.

Concentric

Definition: Circles with the same center.

Example:

The point *O* is center for both circles.

CONGRUENT

Definition: Geometric figures with the same shape and area. Such figures can be superimposed on each other to fit exactly on top of the other.

Symbol: $\cong$

Example:

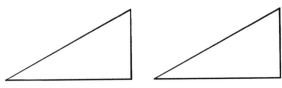

CONJUGATE LAW

Definition: The product of the sum of two numbers and the difference of the same numbers equals the difference of the squares of the two numbers.

Formula: $(a + b)(a - b) = a^2 - b^2$;
            $a + b$ and $a - b$ are called conjugates.

Examples:

1) $(5 + 1)(5 - 1) = 25 - 1 = 24$

2) $(x + 1)(x - 1) = x^2 - 1$

3) $(2x + y)(2x - y) = 4x^2 - y^2$

4) Multiply x + 5 by its conjugate.
   $(x + 5)(x - 5) = x^2 - 25$

Practice: Multiply

a) 81 by 79 by using the conjugate law on
   $(80 + 1)(80 - 1)$.

b) $2a - 1$ by its conjugate.

Consecutive Even Integers

Definition: Every other INTEGER starting with an EVEN NUMBER.

Examples:

1) 2, 4, 6, ...

2) 4, –2, 0, 2, ...

Consecutive Integers

Definition: INTEGERS that follow each other one after the other.

Examples:

1) 1, 2, 3, ...

2) –4, –3, –2, –1, ...

Consecutive Odd Integers

Definition: Every other INTEGER starting with an ODD NUMBER.

Examples:

1) 1, 3, 5, ...

2) –5, –3, –1, ...

Constant

Definition: A number or a symbol that does not change. For example, 5 is always equal to 5 and never more or less; π (PI) is a constant, it is always approximately 3.14.

Examples:

1) In $2x + 3$, 2 and 3 are constants.

2) In ax, a might be a constant.

Constant Term

Definition: A term in an expression that does not contain a VARIABLE.

Examples:

1) In $3x + 2$, 2 is the constant term.

2) In $x^2 + 5x - 4$, -4 is the constant term.

3) In $ax^2 + bx + c$, c is the constant term.

Convex

Definition: Geometric figures where any line segment connecting two points is inside the figure. Compare CONCAVE.

Examples:

1)

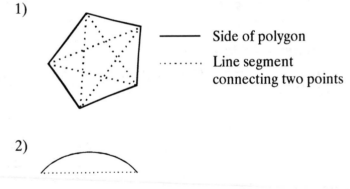

——— Side of polygon

········ Line segment connecting two points

2)

Convex mirror. Outside face is silvered.

Coordinate Geometry

Definition: A system in which graphs with geometric figures are represented by equations.

(It is also called analytic geometry.)

Examples:

1) The graph of the equation $y = x + 2$ is a straight line:
   Point *A* has the COORDINATES (1,3) and satisfies the equation, i.e. $3 = 1 + 2$.
   Point *B* has the coordinates (0,2) and satisfies the equation, i.e. $2 = 0 + 2$.

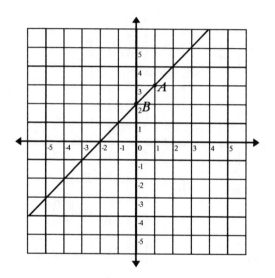

2) An equation in *x* and *y* has a straight line as a graph when the exponents of both *x* and *y* equal 1 (and are therefore not written out). When the exponent of either *x* or *y* (or both) is equal to 2 or more, the graph is a curve.

   The graph of the equation $y = x^2$ is a curve (parabola):

   Point *A* has the coordinates (–2,4) and satisfies the equation, i.e. $4 = (-2)^2$.

   Point *B* has the coordinates (–1, 1) and satisfies the equation, i.e. $1 = (-1)^2$.

Point C has the coordinates $(0,0)$ and satisfies the equation, i.e. $0 = 0^2$.

Point D has the coordinates $(1,1)$ and satisfies the equation, i.e. $1 = 1^2$.

Point E has the coordinates $(2,4)$ and satisfies the equation, i.e. $4 = (2)^2$.

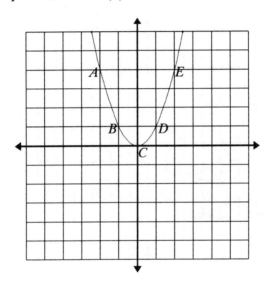

Practice:

Which of the graphs of the following equations is a straight line?

a) $y = x^3$

b) $2x - 3y = 6$

c) $x^2 + y^2 = 9$

COORDINATE PLANE

See CARTESIAN COORDINATE SYSTEM.

COORDINATE SYSTEM

See CARTESIAN COORDINATE SYSTEM.

COORDINATES

Definition: The two numbers in an ORDERED PAIR (x,y). The first number is the x-coordinate; the second number is the y-coordinate.

Examples:

1) In $(5,9)$ the x-coordinate is 5, and the y-coordinate is 9.

2) The x-coordinate of the ORIGIN is 0 and the y-coordinate is also 0. The origin is written as $(0,0)$.

CORRESPONDING (ANGLES OR SIDES)

Definition: Parts of geometric figures that have the same position within each figure.

Symbol: ↔

Examples:

1)

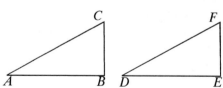

Triangle $ABC \cong$ (is CONGRUENT to) triangle DEF.

$$\angle A \leftrightarrow \angle D \qquad \overline{AB} \leftrightarrow \overline{DE}$$
$$\angle B \leftrightarrow \angle E \qquad \overline{BC} \leftrightarrow \overline{EF}$$
$$\angle C \leftrightarrow \angle F \qquad \overline{AC} \leftrightarrow \overline{DF}$$

2)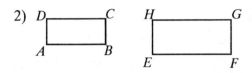

Rectangle *ABCD* is similar to (~) rectangle *EFGH*. The longer sides in the smaller rectangle are corresponding sides to the longer sides in the larger rectangle, and the shorter sides are also corresponding to the shorter sides in the larger rectangle.

COUNTING NUMBERS

Definition: Numbers that are used for counting. These numbers are also called natural numbers or positive integers. (See Appendix 1 on page 19.)

Example:

1, 2, 3, 4, 5, etc.

CROSS MULTIPLICATION

Definition: To multiply cross-wise in a PROPORTION. This is often used to solve equations that can be written as proportions. For example, if nine buttons cost 15 cents, what will four buttons cost? The answer (product) to the multiplication is called the cross product.

Example:

$$\frac{4}{9} = \frac{x}{15}$$

$$\frac{4}{9} \diagdown \frac{x}{15} \qquad 4 \cdot 15 = 9x$$

Practice:

Find the cross product in $\frac{2}{3} = \frac{6}{9}$

Cube

In geometry:

Definition: A solid (three-dimensional) figure with six square FACES.

Examples:

1)

 The volume of a cube with a 2-cm side is
 $(2 \text{ cm})^3 = 2^3 \text{ cm}^3 = 8 \text{ cm}^3$.

2) Each face of the cube in *Example 1* has an area of
 $2^2 \text{ cm}^2 = 4 \text{ cm}^2$.

Practice:

a) Find the total area of the faces of a cube with a side of 1 inch. (Hint: How many faces does a cube have?)

b) Find the volume of a cube with a side of 1 inch.

In exponential notation:

Definition: The third power of a number or variable.

Examples:

1) $2^3 = 2 \times 2 \times 2 = 8$ pronounced "two cubed" or "the cube of two."

2) $x^3 = xxx$ pronounced x cubed or the cube of x.

Practice:

Find the value of 6^3.

Cube Root

Definition: The cube root of a given number is the number that must be raised to the third power to equal the given number.

Symbol: $\sqrt[3]{}$

Examples:

1) The cube root of 8 is 2, because $2^3 = 8$.

2) $\sqrt[3]{27} = 3$, because $3^3 = 27$.

Practice:

Find the cube root of 64.

CUSTOMARY (ENGLISH) SYSTEM OF MEASUREMENT

Definition: Length
   1 mile = 5280 feet
   1 yard = 3 feet
   1 foot = 12 inches

Weight
   1 pound = 16 ounces

Volume
   1 gallon = 4 quarts
   1 quart = 2 pints = 32 fluid ounces
   1 pint = 2 cups
   1 cup = 8 fluid ounces

Examples:

1) 2 gallons = 2 × 4 quarts = 8 quarts

2) 2 gallons = 2 × 4 quarts × 2 pints × 2 cups = 32 cups

3) 1.5 feet = 1.5 × 12 inches = 18 inches

4) 24 inches = 24 ÷ 12 inches per feet = 2 feet

Practice: Convert

a) 1 yard to inches.

b) 3 pounds to ounces.

c) 16 fluid ounces to pints.

DECA-

Definition: A Latin PREFIX in the METRIC SYSTEM standing for 10.

Symbol: da

Example:

1) 1 decameter = 10 meters (1 dam = 10 m)

2) 1 liter = 0.1 decaliters (1 l = 0.1 dal)

Practice:

How many decagrams are there in 10 grams?

DECI-

Definition: A Latin PREFIX in the METRIC SYSTEM equivalent to 0.1.

Symbol: d

Examples:

1) 1 deciliter = 0.1 liters   (1 dl = 0.1 l)

2) 1 meter = 10 decimeters (1 m = 10 dm)

Practice

How many decigrams are there in 10 grams?

DECIMAL NUMBERS

Definition: The DECIMAL SYSTEM is based on the number 10. In this system, numbers with DIGITS to the right of the one's place are called decimal numbers. The digits to the right of the one's place are called decimals. The whole number part is separated from the decimals by a decimal point.

Example:

In 0.123, 0 is the whole number part; 1, 2, and 3 are decimals. This number can also be written as .123.

Decimal numbers are also called decimal fractions, because each decimal can be written as a fraction with a denominator of 10, 100, 1000, etc.

Thus $0.1 = \frac{1}{10}$, $0.01 = \frac{1}{100}$, $0.001 = \frac{1}{1000}$, etc.

Place values: The values of the places after the decimal point follow this order: tenths, hundredths, thousandths, ten-thousandths, and so on. Note, that the names of the places are symmetrical around the ones place: The place one step to the left of one is the tens; two steps to the left of the ones is the hundreds place, etc. One step to the right of the ones place is the tenths place; two steps to the right of the ones is the hundredths place, etc. (See the following diagram, which illustrates the places of the number 3454.159.)

3	4	5	4 .	1	5	9
thousands	hundreds	tens	ones	tenths	hundredths	thousandths

Examples:

1) In 0.123, 1 has a value of $\frac{1}{10}$, 2 has a value of $\frac{2}{100}$, and 3 has a value of $\frac{3}{1000}$.

2) In 10.02, 2 has a value of two hundredths.

Reading Decimal Numbers: The digits to the left of the decimal point are read as whole numbers, the decimal point is read as "and," and the digits to the right of the decimal point are read as a whole number followed by the name of the decimal place value furthest to the right.

Examples:

1) 1.23 is read as "one and 23 hundredths."
   We can also read it as "one point two, three."

2) 0.0025 is read as "25 ten-thousandths."
   or " point, zero, zero, two, five."

Practice:

Write the following in words:

a) 45.01

b) 0.105

Decimals are classified into the following groups:

Terminating decimals:

Decimals numbers that end with the last digit.

Example:

0.125

Nonterminating decimals:

Decimal numbers that never end.

Symbol: ...

Example:

1.414213...

Repeating decimals:

Decimal numbers that have repeating groups.

Example:

0.121212... (The repeating group is 12.)

Nonrepeating decimals:

Decimal numbers that have no repeating groups.

Examples:

1) 1.414213...

2) 3.141592... (This is PI.)

Conversions:

Decimals to fractions: The decimal number is written in fractional form and REDUCED if possible.

Examples:

1) 0.15 = fifteen hundredths = $\dfrac{15}{100} = \dfrac{3}{20}$

2) 1.3 = one and three tenths = $1\dfrac{3}{10}$

Practice:

Convert 32.125 to a common fraction.

Fractions to decimals:

Examples:

1) $\dfrac{4}{5} = 4 \div 5 = 0.8$

2) $3\dfrac{4}{5} = 3.8$

Practice:

Convert $1\dfrac{1}{4}$ to decimals.

Decimals to percents: Multiplying by 100 will move the decimal point two places to the right and give you a percent. See POWERS OF 10.

Examples:

1) $0.25 = 25\%$

2) $0.003 = 0.3\%$

Practice:

Convert 1.25 to percents.

Percents to decimals: Dividing by 100 will move the decimal point 2 steps to the left and give you a decimal. (Drop the percent symbol.)

Examples:

1) 25% = 0.25

2) 0.002% = 0.00002

Practice:

Convert 250% to a decimal number.

Operations:

Addition and Subtraction: Align numbers one below another by their decimal points. Proceed as with whole numbers.

Examples:

1) Add 4.35 and 0.4.

$$\begin{array}{r} 4.35 \\ +\ 0.4 \\ \hline 4.75 \end{array}$$

2) Add 15.23 and 2.

$$\begin{array}{r} 15.23 \\ +\ 2. \\ \hline 17.23 \end{array}$$

3) Subtract 5.93 from 7.04.

$$\begin{array}{r} 7.04 \\ -\ 5.93 \\ \hline 1.11 \end{array}$$

4) Subtract 5 from 16.35.

$$\begin{array}{r} 16.35 \\ -\ 5. \\ \hline 11.35 \end{array}$$

Practice:

a) Add 4.53 and .45.

b) Subtract 3.8 from 6.

Multiplication: Multiply the numbers without regard to the decimals. The sum of the decimal places is the number of decimal places in the product.

Examples:

1) $4.5 \times 1.2 = 45 \times 12$ (2 decimal places)
   $= 540$ (2 decimal places) $= 5.40$

2) $0.003 \times 0.0001 = 3$ (7 decimal places) $= 0.0000003$

Practice:

Multiply 5.6×0.1

Division: The DIVISOR is made a whole number by moving the decimal point to the right. Move the decimal point in the DIVIDEND the same number of places. Mark the decimal point and proceed as with LONG DIVISION of whole numbers.

Examples:

1) $4.5 \div 3$ Here we do not have to change the divisor since it is a whole number already.

$$
\begin{array}{r}
1.5 \\
3\overline{)4.5} \\
\underline{-3} \\
15 \\
\underline{-15} \\
0
\end{array}
$$

2) $5.13 \div 0.3$

$$
0.3\overline{)5.13} \Rightarrow 3\overline{)51.3} \Rightarrow
\begin{array}{r}
17.1 \\
3\overline{)51.3} \\
\underline{-3} \\
21 \\
\underline{-21} \\
3 \\
\underline{-3} \\
0
\end{array}
$$

Practice:

Divide 14.25 ÷ 0.05

Multiplication and division by powers of 10: To multiply a number by 10 raised to a whole number, move the decimal point to the right the same number of places as the value of the exponent.

Example:

$0.0356 \times 10^5 = 3560$

To divide a number by 10 raised to a whole number, move the decimal point to the left the same number of places as the exponent. See also POWERS OF 10.

Example:

$5782 \div 10^3 = 5.782$

Rounding of Decimals: See ROUNDING.

Comparing (Ordering) Decimals: Arrange the numbers in a column with the decimal points below each other. Compare the place values going from left to right.

Example:

0.095 is smaller than 0.6.
    0.6
    0.095
6 > 0 (is greater than)
Alternate solution: Write 0.6 as 0.600. Then compare 600 thousandths and 95 thousandths.

Practice:

Arrange the numbers 1.2, 0.876 and 0.00999 in order from the smallest to the largest.

DECIMAL POINT

Definition: A point to show where the whole number ends. The decimal point is read as "and" or simply "point."

Example: 14.25

DECIMAL SYSTEM

Definition: A number system based on the number 10. In this system 10 DIGITS are used: 0, 1, 2, 3, 4, 5, 6, 7, 8, and 9. The position of the digit in the number gives the value of the digit. See also PLACE VALUE.

Examples:

1) In 250, the digit 2 has a value of 200.

2) In 12,345, the digit 2 has a value of 2000.

3) In 3.526, the digit 2 has a value of 0.02 or "two tenths."

Practice:

In 607.82, what is the value of each digit?

DECREASE

Definition: Make smaller.

Example:

To decrease 15 by 3, subtract 3 from 15. 15 − 3 = 12

DEGREE

In temperature:

Definition: A unit of temperature. (See also TEMPERATURE.) In the Customary (English) system the unit is called Fahrenheit. In the metric system the unit is called Celsius (formerly called centigrade). $1°C = 1.8°F$

Symbol: °

Examples:

1) Water freezes at 32° Fahrenheit.

2) Water freezes at 0° Celsius.

In geometry:

Definition: A unit of measure of angles.

Symbol: °

Examples:

1) A right angle measures 90°.

2) An acute ANGLE measures between 0° and 90°.

In geography:

Definition: A unit of measuring latitude and longitude.

Example:

New York City lies at 41° latitude and 74° longitude.

In algebra:

Definition: The exponent of a variable or the highest power of an expression.

Examples:

1) x^5 has a degree of 5.

2) The degree of the expression $x^3 + 2x - 5$ is 3.

DENOMINATOR

Definition: The bottom part of a FRACTION. It can never equal zero, because fractions are a form of division and we cannot divide by zero.

Example

In $\frac{3}{4}$, 4 is the denominator.

DEPENDENT VARIABLE

Definition: The variable (usually y) that depends on another independent variable (usually x).

Example:

> If you choose different values for x in the equation $y = 5x$, the value of y becomes 5 times each value of x.
> If x is 1, y is 5; if x is 2, y is 10; if x is 3, y is 15; etc.

DIAGONAL

Definition: A line segment joining two VERTICES of a polygon that are not next to each other.

Example:

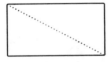

············ is the diagonal.

DIAMETER

Definition: The distance across a CIRCLE through its center. The diameter is twice the RADIUS. All of the straight dotted lines in the figure are diameters.

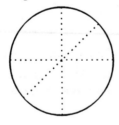

Example:

> If the radius of a circle is 3 inches, the diameter is 6 inches.

DIFFERENCE

Definition: The answer in a subtraction problem.

Example:

The difference of 6 and 4 is 2. $6 - 4 = 2$

DIGITS

Definition: The symbols 0, 1, 2, 3, 4, 5, 6, 7, 8, and 9.

Example:

459 is a three-digit number.

DISTANCE

In MOTION PROBLEMS:

Definition: A measure of how far something travels.

Formula: distance = rate × time (See also RATE.)

Example:

If an automobile travels 50 mph for 3 hours, it has traveled 150 miles.
$d = rt$
$d = 50 \times 3 = 150$
Answer: 150 miles

In geometry:

Definition: The length of the straight path between two points. If both points lie on the x-axis and are called a and b, the distance between a and b is the absolute value $|a - b|$ (or $|b - a|$).

Example:

The distance between -4 and 3 is $|-4 - 3| = |-7| = 7$.

If both points are anywhere in a plane, the distance between them is found by using the distance formula.

Formula: Call the points (x_1, y_1) and (x_2, y_2).

The distance $d = \sqrt{(x_1 - x_2)^2 + (y_1 - y_2)^2}$

The distance formula is based on the PYTHAGOREAN THEOREM, which states that $a^2 + b^2 = c^2$, where a, b, and c are the sides of a right triangle.

In the diagram, the short sides of the triangle are 3, and 4 units. d is the longest side in the triangle.

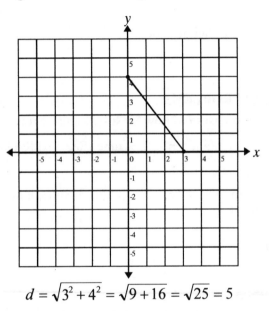

$$d = \sqrt{3^2 + 4^2} = \sqrt{9 + 16} = \sqrt{25} = 5$$

Examples:

1) The distance between the points $(-4,0)$ and $(3,0)$ is
$$\sqrt{(-4-3)^2 + (0-0)^2} = \sqrt{49} = 7$$

2) The distance between the points $(2,3)$ and $(6,6)$ is
$$\sqrt{(2-6)^2 + (3-6)^2} = \sqrt{16+9} = \sqrt{25} = 5$$

3) The distance between the points $(-2,1)$ and $(3,4)$ is
$$\sqrt{(-2-3)^2 + (1-4)^2} = \sqrt{25+9} = \sqrt{34}$$

Practice:

Find the distance between the points (1,5) and (13,10).

DISTRIBUTIVE PROPERTY

Definition: The rules of the ORDER OF OPERATIONS state that the inside of any grouping symbols such as parentheses must be simplified before a multiplication can take place. However, this can be avoided by multiplying *each* term in the additions or subtractions inside the parentheses. This is called distribution of the multiplication over addition and subtraction.

Formulas: $a(b + c) = ab + ac$

$a(b - c) = ab - ac$

This property (also called principle, rule, or law) is used mostly in algebra to simplify certain expressions or to revise the procedure—that is, $ab + ac = a(b + c)$—in FACTORING out a common factor. The distributive property can also be used in mental arithmetic. For example, 53×12 can be rewritten as $53(10 + 2) = 53 \times 10 + 53 \times 2 = 530 + 106 = 636$.

Examples:

1) $5(2 + 4) = 5(2) + 5(4)$

2) $3x(4 - x) = 12x - 3x^2$

Practice:

Multiply mentally 99×15 by using "distribution over subtraction."

DIVIDEND

Definition: The number that will be divided.

Example:

$12 \div 4$ or $4\overline{)12}$.   12 is the dividend.

DIVISIBILITY RULES

Definition: Shortcuts to determine when a number can be divided by certain other numbers. Numbers that are divisible by

Two:	All even numbers.
Three:	The sum of the digits is divisible by three.
Five:	The number ends in 0 or 5.

Examples:

1) 54 is divisible by 2 and 3 (5 + 4 = 9). 54 is an even number and the sum of its digits is divisible by 3.

2) 30 is divisible by 2, 3, and 5 (as well as 6, 10 and 15).

Practice:

a) Which of the following numbers are divisible by 2: 111, 112, 113, 114?

b) By 3?

DIVISION

Definition: Repeated subtraction. The reverse of multiplication. See also DIVIDEND and DIVISOR.

Symbols: $\div$, /, — (fraction bar), $\overline{)}$

Example:

12 ÷ 4 = 3 because 12 − 4 − 4 − 4 = 0.
We also have 4 × 3 = 12.

DIVISOR

Definition: The number to divide by.

Example:

In 12 ÷ 4 or $4\overline{)12}$ 4 is the divisor.

EDGE

Definition: A line segment that separates the FACES of a solid figure.

Example:

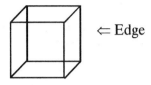 ⇐ Edge

A cube has 12 edges.

ELIMINATION METHOD

A method of solving equations with more than one variable (SIMULTANEOUS EQUATIONS). Two variables require two equations. One variable is eliminated when the equations are added. This method is also called the ADDITION METHOD.

ENGLISH STANDARD SYSTEM OF MEASUREMENT

This system of measurements is the one used in the United States and uses inches, feet, yards, ounces, pounds, etc. It is usually called the CUSTOMARY SYSTEM.

EQUATION

Definition: A statement that two expressions are equal. An equation always contains an equal sign.

Examples:

1) $2 + 3 = 5$ (This equation has only numbers and is called a NUMERICAL EQUATION.)

2) $2x + 3 = 5$ (This equation contains a VARIABLE and can be solved. It is called an ALGEBRAIC EQUATION.)

See also LINEAR EQUATIONS, QUADRATIC EQUA-TIONS, SIMULTANEOUS EQUATIONS and SOLVING EQUATIONS.

Practice:

Which of the following are equations?

a) $3x + 5$

b) $11 - 8 = 3$

c) $3x + 5 = 2$

EQUILATERAL TRIANGLE

Definition: A triangle with equal sides. All angles are 60°.

Example:

If the PERIMETER of an equilateral triangle is 30 cm, all sides are 10 cm. ($30 \div 3 = 10$)

EQUIVALENT EQUATIONS

Definition: Equations that have the same solution.

Example:

$2x - 4 = 2$ and $2x = 6$ both have the solution $x = 3$.

EQUIVALENT FRACTIONS

Definition: FRACTIONS that have the same value. See also FRACTIONS.

Example:

$$\frac{1}{2} = \frac{4}{8}$$

ESTIMATION

Definition: An APPROXIMATION or educated guess of the final answer.

Example:

$453 + 687 \approx 500 + 700 \approx 1200$
($\approx$ means approximately equal to.)

EVALUATE

Definition: The word means to calculate the answer in an arithmetic expression. See also ORDER OF OPERATIONS. It also means to find the value of an ALGEBRAIC EXPRESSION when the variables are exchanged for numbers.

Examples:

1) $3^2 \times 3^3 = 9 \times 27 = 243$

2) $2a + b$ for $a = -1$ and $b = 2$ is $2(-1) + 2 = -2 + 2 = 0$

Practice: Evaluate

a) $3 + 2 \times 4$
Remember that multiplication goes before addition!

b) $3x^2 + 4x + 5$ for $x = 2$

EVEN NUMBER

Definition: The set of numbers divisible by 2.

Example:

The set of even numbers is $\{2, 4, 6, 8, ...\}$.

EXACT NUMBER

Definition: A number that is not ROUNDED.

Example:

4.0 can be written as 4, 4.00, 4.000, etc.

Expanded Form

Definition: A number that is written as the sum of each digit multiplied by its PLACE VALUE. The place value can be written as 10, 100, 1000, etc., or in EXPONENTIAL NOTATION, $10, 10^2, 10^3$, etc.

Examples:

1) $4523 = 4 \times 1000 + 5 \times 100 + 2 \times 10 + 3 \times 1$ (The " $\times 1$ " is usually skipped.)

2) $4523 = 4 \times 10^3 + 5 \times 10^2 + 2 \times 10 + 3$

3) $1.257 = 1 + 2 \times 10^{-1} + 5 \times 10^{-2} + 7 \times 10^{-3}$

Practice:

Write 50, 391 in expanded notation.

Exponent

Definition: A number or symbol that indicates a repeated multiplication. It is written as a superscript to the right and above the BASE (the number that is multiplied by itself). See also POWER.

Examples:

1) In 2^5, 5 is the exponent, 2 is the base and is multiplied by itself four times. That is, the base is multiplied by itself (exponent $- 1$) times.
$2^5 = 2 \times 2 \times 2 \times 2 \times 2 = 32$

2) In a^b, b is the exponent.

The exponent is a natural number:

Definition: The number tells how many FACTORS (the number repeated in the multiplication) of one kind (the base) there are. People often say that the number is multiplied by itself that many times, but that is not correct. There are one less multiplication symbols than factors.

Examples:

1) $5^2 = 5 \times 5 = 25$ 2 factors, one multiplication

2) $a^6 = aaaaaa\ (= a \times a \times a \times a \times a \times a)$
   6 factors, 5 multiplications

Practice: Find the value of:

a) 3^4

b) 4^3

The exponent is 0:

Definition: Any number with an exponent of 0 is equal to 1. (See explanation under *Division Example 4* below.) The exception to the rule is 0^0, which is undefined.

Examples:

1) $5^0 = 1$

2) $3^0 = 1$

Practice:

Find the value of 10^0.

The exponent is a negative number:

Definition: A number with a negative exponent is INVERTED (1 divided by the number) and the negative exponent becomes positive.

Formula: $a^{-b} = \dfrac{1}{a^b}$

Examples:

1) $2^{-1} = \dfrac{1}{2^{+1}} = \dfrac{1}{2}$

2) $3^{-2} = \dfrac{1}{3^2} = \dfrac{1}{9}$

3) $\dfrac{1}{5^{-3}} = 5^3 = 125$

Practice:

Rewrite 2^{-5} with a positive exponent.

The exponent is a fraction:

Definition: A number with a fractional exponent can be re-written in RADICAL form (root form). The denominator of the fraction becomes the INDEX of the radical. When the index equals 2, it represents a square root and only the radical is written.

Formula: $\qquad a^{b/c} = \sqrt[c]{a^b}$

Examples:

1) $5^{1/2} = \sqrt{5}$ The square root has an index of 2, which is not written out.

2) $32^{1/5} = \sqrt[5]{32} = 2$

3) $4^{3/2} = \sqrt{4^3} = \sqrt{64} = 8$

Practice:

Rewrite $49^{1/2}$ in radical form.

Operations:

Addition and subtraction: If the bases are the same and the exponents are the same, add or subtract the COEFFICIENTS. This is also called combining like terms. If this is not possible, EVALUATE.

Examples:

1) $3ab^2 + 5ab^2 = 8ab^2$

2) $5^3 + 5^3 = 2(5^3) = 250$

3) $2^2 + 2 = 4 + 2 = 6$

Practice: Add or subtract

a) $3x^2 + 8x^2$

b) $a^2 + a^2$

c) $3^2 - 3$

Multiplication: To multiply terms having the same base, add the exponents. When multiplying algebraic terms, *multiply* coefficients and *add* exponents.

Examples:

1) $7^2 \cdot 7^5 = 7^7$

2) $x^2 x^4 = x^6$

3) $2a^5 \cdot 3a^8 = 6a^{13}$

Practice:

Multiply: $5^2 a^3 \cdot 5^6 a^7$

Division: *Divide* coefficients and *subtract* exponents of the numerator and the denominator (provided the bases are the same).

Examples:

1) $\dfrac{5^6}{5^4} = 5^2$

2) $25x^3 y^5 \div 5x^2 y^3 = 5x^{3-2}\, y^{5-3} = 5xy^2$

3) $\dfrac{3^2}{6} = \dfrac{9}{6} = \dfrac{3}{2}$

4) $\dfrac{3^2}{3^2} = \dfrac{9}{9} = 1$, but $\dfrac{3^2}{3^2} = 3^{2-2} = 3^0$

This proves that any number raised to the power of 0 equals 1.

Practice:

Divide $42x^2 y^7 \div 7x^2 y^3$

Powers: When a number in exponential form, such as a^b, is raised to a power, such as c, multiply the exponents.

Formula: If a, b, and c represent any numbers, then $(a^b)^c = a^{bc}$.

91

Examples:

1) $(5^2)^3 = 5^6$

2) $(x^5)^9 = x^{45}$

Practice:

Find the value of $(2^3)^2$ by using the formula and then calculate by hand or using your calculator if it has a key x^y or y^x. Then do the calculation again by first determining the value of what is inside the parentheses and then square the answer.

Formula: If a, b, and c represent any numbers, then $(ab)^c = a^c b^c$.

When a product is raised to a power, each factor is raised to that power.

Examples:

1) $(2 \cdot 3)^3 = 2^3 \cdot 3^3 = 8 \cdot 27 = 216$

2) $(5x^2)^3 = 5^3 x^6 = 125x^6$

Practice:

Use the formula to find the answer to $(2 \cdot 5)^3$ and then solve the problem again by first calculating what is inside the parentheses and then raising the answer to the third power.

EXPONENTIAL NOTATION
See EXPONENT.

EXPRESSION
Definition: Any combination of symbols and operations.

Examples:

1) Numerical expression: $3 + 5 \times 6 - 8 \div 2$

2) Algebraic expression: $5x^2 + 6x - 9y$

Face

Definition: A plane surface on a solid.

Example:

A cube has six square faces.

Factor

Whole number:

Definition: A number that divides a whole number evenly. A number has always 1 and itself as factors. Any number that has *only* 1 and itself as factors is called a PRIME NUMBER.

Example:

2 and 3 are factors of 6 because $6 \div 2 = 3$ and $6 \div 3 = 2$. $6 = 2 \times 3$ is written in factored form.

Algebraic expression:

Definition: A number, variable, or algebraic expression that divides an algebraic expression evenly. See also FACTORING.

Examples:

1) x and $x + 1$ are factors of $x^2 + x$, because

$$\frac{x^2 + x}{x} = \frac{x^2}{x} + \frac{x}{x} = x + 1$$

2) $(x + 2)$ and $(x + 3)$ are factors of $x^2 + 5x + 6$, because $(x + 2)(x + 3) = x^2 + 5x + 6$.

Factor Tree

Definition: A way of showing how a number is FACTORED into PRIME FACTORS. It does not matter how we start to factor a number as long as we continue factoring until all factors are prime numbers.

Example:

24 is factored as follows:

```
        24
       /  \
      4    6
     /\   /\
    2  2 2  3
```

$24 = 2 \times 2 \times 2 \times 3$

Practice:

Make a factor tree for the factoring of 24 starting with the factors 2 and 12.

FACTORING (FACTORIZATION)

Definition: To change a number or an expression into a multiplication. This is of importance especially at the precalculus and calculus levels.

Examples:

1) $24 = 4 \times 6$

2) $3x^2 + 6x = 3(x^2 + 2x)$ Compare with *factor completely* section on the following page.

3) $x^2 + 5x + 6 = (x + 2)(x + 3)$ See FOIL.

Factor into prime factors. Continue to factor until all factors are prime numbers (that is, numbers that are not divisible by any other number than one and itself). Use a FACTOR TREE, if that is helpful.

Examples:

1) $12 = 4 \times 3 = 2 \times 2 \times 3$

2) $36 = 6 \times 6 = 2 \times 3 \times 2 \times 3 = 2^2 \times 3^2$

Practice:

Factor 50 into prime factors.

Factor completely. Factor an algebraic expression as far as possible by factoring out the GREATEST COMMON FACTOR. If the greatest common factor (the largest factor) is not obvious to begin with, factor in steps.

Example:

1) $3x^2 + 6x = 3(x^2 + 2x) = 3x(x + 2)$ Both 3 and x are common factors, but $3x$ is the greatest common factor.

2) $10x^3 + 30x^2 + 40x + 20 = 10(x^3 + 3x^2 + 4x + 2)$

3) $x(x - 1) + 2(x - 1) = (x - 1)(x + 2)$

Practice:

Factor as far as possible: $3x^4 + 6x^3 + 9x^2 - 21x$

Factor a polynomial. Follow these steps:

Step 1. Factor out the GREATEST COMMON FACTOR (GCF):

Examples:

1) $9x^2 - 81 = 9(x^2 - 9)$; 3 and 9 are both common factors, but 9 is the GCF.

2) $5x^3 - 25x^2 + 15x = 5x(x^2 - 5x + 3)$; 5 and x are both common factors, but $5x$ is the GCF.

Practice:

Find the greatest common factor in
a) $6x^2 + 12xy$

b) $10xy^2 - 20x^2y$

Step 2. When the greatest common factor has been factored out, there remains a second factor, which might be factored. If this second factor is a difference between two squares, it can be factored according to the CONJUGATE LAW.

Formula: $a^2 - b^2 = (a - b)(a + b)$

Note, the sum of two squares cannot be factored.

Examples:

    1) $x^2 - 9 = (x + 3)(x - 3)$

    2) $4x^2 - 25 = (2x + 5)(2x - 5)$

Practice: Factor

    a) $9x^2 - 16$

    b) $3x^2 - 12$

If the second factor is the difference between two cubes, it can be factored according to the following formula.

Formula: $a^3 - b^3 = (a - b)(a^2 + ab + b^2)$

Example:

    $x^3 - 27 = x^3 - 3^3 = (x - 3)(x^2 + 3x + 9)$

Practice: Factor

    a) $x^3 - 64$

    b) $8x^3 - 64$ Make sure to factor <u>completely</u>!

If the second factor is the sum of two cubes, it can be factored according to the following formula.

Formula: $a^3 + b^3 = (a + b)(a^2 - ab + b^2)$

Example:

    $x^3 + 8 = x^3 + 2^3 = (x + 2)(x^2 - 2x + 4)$

Practice:

    Factor $8x^3 + 27$

If the second factor is a TRINOMIAL, it can often be factored into two BINOMIALS. Since factoring is the reverse of multiplication, we can take two binomials, multiply them, and examine the resulting trinomial. Take for example, $(x + 1)(x + 2)$ and multiply according to the FOIL method.

$$(x + 1)(x + 2) = x^2 + 2x + x + 2 = x^2 + 3x + 2$$

Note, that $3 = 1 + 2$; in other words the coefficient for x is the sum of the constant terms in the factored form. The constant term in the trinomial is the product of the constant terms in the factors. You can—and always should—check your work by multiplying the binomials.

Formula: $x^2 + bx + c = (x + d)(x + e)$,
where $d + e = b$ and $de = c$.

Examples:

1) Factor the trinomial into two binomials.
   $x^2 + 7x + 12 = (x + 3)(x + 4)$
   To check: $3 + 4 = 7$ and $3(4) = 12$

2) Factor the trinomial into two binomials.
   $x^2 - 2x - 24 = (x - 6)(x + 4)$
   To check: $-6 + 4 = -2$ and $-6(4) = -24$

Practice: Factor

   a) $x^2 + 8x + 15$

   b) $x^2 - 2x - 15$

To factor a trinomial where the coefficient for x^2 does not equal 1, one has to guess. In other words: $ax^2 + bx + c$, where $a \neq 1$ can only be factored by trial and error.

Examples:

   1) $2x^2 + 11x + 12 = (2x + 3)(x + 4)$

   2) $5x^2 - 7x - 6 = (5x + 3)(x - 2)$

Practice: Factor

   a) $3x^2 + 7x + 2$

   b) $3x^2 + 5x - 2$

FAHRENHEIT

Definition: A unit of temperature. See also TEMPERATURE.

Symbol: $^{\circ}F$

Examples:

1) Water freezes at $32^{\circ}F$ ($0^{\circ}C$).

2) Water boils at $212^{\circ}F$ ($100^{\circ}C$).

FOIL

Definition: A method to multiply two BINOMIALS. F stands for FIRST, O stands for OUTER, I stands for INNER, and L stands for LAST.

Formula: $\quad (a + b)(c + d) = ac + ad + bc + bd$
$$\qquad\qquad\qquad\quad\ \ \text{F}\quad\ \ \text{O}\quad\ \ \text{I}\quad\ \ \text{L}$$

Examples:

1) $(x + 1)(x + 2) = x^2 + 2x + x + 2 = x^2 + 3x + 2$

2) $(5x - 3)(2x + 7) = 10x^2 + 35x - 6x - 21$
$$= 10x^2 + 29x - 21$$

Practice: Multiply

a) $(x - 3)(x + 3)$

b) $(2x - 5)(3x + 4)$

FRACTION BAR

Definition: The dividing line between the NUMERATOR and the DENOMINATOR. The fraction bar means division.

Examples:

1) $\dfrac{4}{5} \Leftarrow$ fraction bar

2) $^4\!/_5$

FRACTIONS

Definitions:

Fraction: An INTEGER divided by another integer. The second integer cannot equal 0, because one cannot divide by 0. The first number is called the numerator and the second number the denominator. The division symbol is a fraction bar (—) or sometimes a slash (/).

Example:

$$\frac{5}{7}, \frac{12}{2}, \frac{0}{4}, \frac{8}{-3}, \frac{-5}{7}, -\frac{4}{5}, \text{ and } \frac{1}{2}$$

Common fraction: The same as fraction.

Proper fraction: The numerator is smaller than the denominator.

Example: $\frac{5}{9}$

Improper fraction: The numerator is larger than the denominator.

Example: $\frac{15}{2}$

Mixed number: An integer followed by a proper fraction.

Example: $4\frac{1}{5}$

Equivalent fractions: Fractions with the same value.

Examples:

1) $\frac{1}{2} = \frac{4}{8}$

2) $\frac{5}{6} = \frac{10}{12}$

3) $\frac{25}{30} = \frac{5}{6}$

Reduce a fraction: Divide numerator and denominator by a common FACTOR. This is a special case of **equivalent fractions**.

Example:

$$\frac{12}{16} = \frac{6}{8}$$ Here the common factor of 12 and 16 is 2.

Reduce to lowest terms: Reduce a fraction so the numerator and the denominator have no common factors.

Example:

$$\frac{6}{8} = \frac{3}{4}$$ The common factor of 6 and 8 is again 2.

But 3 and 4 have no common factor.

Complex fraction: The numerator or the denominator or both are fractions. Re-write the complex fractions as division of fractions. (See Operations.)

Examples:

1) $$\frac{\frac{3}{4}}{3} = \frac{3}{4} \div 3 = \frac{3}{4} \times \frac{1}{3} = \frac{1}{4}$$

2) $$\frac{\frac{4}{5}}{\frac{2}{15}} = \frac{4}{5} \div \frac{2}{15} = \frac{4}{5} \times \frac{15}{2} = \frac{60}{10} = 6$$

Conversions:

To convert an **improper fraction to a mixed number:** Divide the numerator by the denominator. The REMAINDER is the new numerator.

Example: $\frac{15}{4} = 3\frac{3}{4}$

To convert a **mixed number to an improper fraction:** Multiply the whole number by the denominator. Add the numerator. This is the new numerator. Keep the same denominator.

Example: $4\frac{1}{5} = \frac{4 \times 5 + 1}{5} = \frac{21}{5}$

To convert **fractions to decimals:** Divide the numerator by the denominator.

Examples:

1) $\frac{4}{5} = 4 \div 5 = 0.8$ (Use long division or the calculator.)

2) $3\frac{4}{5} = 3.8$ (The whole number part stays the same.)

To convert **decimals to fractions:** Write out the decimal number as it is read. Reduce if possible.

Examples:

1) $0.03 = \frac{3}{100}$

2) $1.25 = 1\frac{25}{100} = 1\frac{1}{4}$

To convert **percents to fractions:** Divide by 100; drop the percent symbol.

Examples:

1) $75\% = \frac{75}{100} = \frac{3}{4}$

2) $33\frac{1}{3}\% = \frac{100}{3} \div 100 = \frac{100}{3} \times \frac{1}{100} = \frac{100}{300} = \frac{1}{3}$

3) $\frac{1}{2}\% = \frac{1}{2} \div 100 = \frac{1}{2} \times \frac{1}{100} = \frac{1}{200}$

To convert **fractions to percents:** Multiply by 100%.

Examples:

1) $\frac{1}{2} = \frac{1}{2} \times 100\% = \frac{100}{2}\% = 50\%$

2) $\dfrac{1}{3} = \dfrac{1}{3} \times 100\% = \dfrac{100}{3}\% = 33\dfrac{1}{3}\%$

3) $2\dfrac{1}{5} = \dfrac{11}{5} \times 100\% = \dfrac{1100}{5}\% = 220\%$

Operations:

Addition and Subtraction: To add or subtract fractions with the same denominators, add or subtract the numerators and keep the denominators. You may change mixed numbers to improper fractions before you subtract.

Examples:

1) $\dfrac{1}{5} + \dfrac{2}{5} = \dfrac{3}{5}$

2) $5\dfrac{1}{6} - 3\dfrac{5}{6} = \dfrac{31}{6} - \dfrac{23}{6} = \dfrac{8}{6} = \dfrac{4}{3} = 1\dfrac{1}{3}$

Practice:

Add or subtract:

a) $\dfrac{7}{8} - \dfrac{3}{8}$

b) $4\dfrac{2}{5} + 2\dfrac{3}{5}$

To add or subtract fractions with different denominators, rewrite the fractions as equivalent fractions with common denominators. Then follow the rule for addition and subtraction of fractions with the same denominators.

Examples:

1) $\dfrac{1}{3} + \dfrac{1}{2} = \dfrac{2}{6} + \dfrac{3}{6} = \dfrac{5}{6}$

2) $\dfrac{4}{5} - \dfrac{2}{3} = \dfrac{12}{15} - \dfrac{10}{15} = \dfrac{2}{15}$

Practice:

Add or subtract:

a) $\dfrac{2}{5} + \dfrac{3}{10}$

b) $\dfrac{5}{9} - \dfrac{1}{6}$

Subtracting with borrowing:

Borrow 1 and write it as $\dfrac{a}{a}$, if a is the desired denominator. For example, $1 = \dfrac{2}{2} = \dfrac{3}{3} = \dfrac{4}{4} = \dfrac{5}{5}$, etc.

Examples:

1) $5\dfrac{1}{6} - 3\dfrac{5}{6}$

$$5\dfrac{1}{6} = 4 + 1\dfrac{1}{6} = 4 + \dfrac{6+1}{6} = 4\dfrac{7}{6}$$

$$-3\dfrac{5}{6} = \qquad\qquad\qquad -3\dfrac{5}{6}$$

$$\qquad\qquad\qquad\qquad 1\dfrac{2}{6} = 1\dfrac{1}{3}$$

2) $3 - 1\dfrac{1}{5}$

$$3 = 2 + 1 = 2\dfrac{5}{5}$$

$$-1\dfrac{1}{5} = \qquad -1\dfrac{1}{5}$$

$$\qquad\qquad 1\dfrac{4}{5}$$

Practice:

Subtract:

a) $1 - \dfrac{3}{5}$

b) $4\dfrac{1}{3} - 2\dfrac{2}{3}$

103

Multiplication: Multiply the numerators and multiply the denominators. Mixed numbers must be changed to improper fractions before they can be multiplied.

Examples:

1) $\frac{2}{3} \times \frac{3}{5} = \frac{6}{15}$ or $\frac{2}{5}$

2) $2\frac{1}{3} \times 3\frac{3}{7} = \frac{7}{3} \times \frac{24}{7} = \frac{1 \times 8}{1 \times 1} = \frac{8}{1} = 8$

   Note that the fractions were reduced by 7 and 3.

Practice:

Multiply

a) $\frac{1}{7} \times \frac{2}{7}$

b) $1\frac{1}{2} \times 4\frac{2}{3}$

Division: Multiply by the RECIPROCAL (the inverted form) of the DIVISOR. Mixed numbers must be changed to improper fractions before they can be inverted.

Examples:

1) $\frac{2}{5} \div \frac{4}{15} = \frac{2}{5} \times \frac{15}{4} = \frac{30}{20} = \frac{3}{2} = 1\frac{1}{2}$

2) $2\frac{5}{8} \div 1\frac{2}{5} = \frac{21}{8} \div \frac{7}{5} = \frac{21}{8} \times \frac{5}{7} = \frac{3 \times 5}{8} = \frac{15}{8} = 1\frac{7}{8}$

Practice:

Divide

a) $\frac{3}{7} \div \frac{1}{7}$

b) $3\frac{1}{3} \div 2\frac{1}{2}$

Powers: Raise both the numerator and the denominator to the indicated POWER. Change a mixed number to an improper fraction before raising to the power.

Examples:

1) $\left(\dfrac{2}{3}\right)^4 = \dfrac{2^4}{3^4} = \dfrac{16}{81}$

2) $\left(2\dfrac{1}{2}\right)^3 = \left(\dfrac{5}{2}\right)^3 = \dfrac{125}{8}$

Practice:

Raise to the indicated power and leave the answer as fractions without exponents.

a) $\left(\dfrac{1}{2}\right)^5$

b) $\left(2\dfrac{3}{5}\right)^3$

Ordering Fractions: Change the fractions to equivalent fractions with the same denominators. Then compare the numerators. The fractions can also be changed to decimals and compared.

Examples:

1) $\dfrac{5}{11}$ is smaller than $\dfrac{7}{11}$.

The denominators are the same, so you compare the numerators.

$5 < 7$, so $\dfrac{5}{11} < \dfrac{7}{11}$.

2) From the smallest to the largest, the order of the following list is $\dfrac{5}{7}, \dfrac{2}{3}$, and $\dfrac{7}{9}$.

The LEAST COMMON DENOMINATOR is 63.

$$\frac{5}{7} = \frac{45}{63}$$

$$\frac{2}{3} = \frac{42}{63}$$

$$\frac{7}{9} = \frac{49}{63}$$

$42 < 45 < 49$, so $\frac{2}{3} < \frac{5}{7} < \frac{7}{9}$

3) Change the following fractions to decimals and put them in order from the smallest to the largest:

$\frac{2}{5}, \frac{1}{3}, \frac{3}{7}$, and $\frac{5}{13}$.

$$\frac{2}{5} = 0.40$$

$$\frac{1}{3} = 0.333...$$

$$\frac{3}{7} = 0.42857... \approx 0.43$$

$$\frac{5}{13} = 0.3846... \approx 0.38$$

We can order the decimal fractions by looking at the first two decimals. Thus $0.33 < 0.38 < 0.40 < 0.43$

and $\frac{1}{3} < \frac{5}{13} < \frac{2}{5} < \frac{3}{7}$

Practice:

Determine which is smaller

a) $\frac{2}{3}$ or $\frac{8}{13}$

b) $\frac{1}{7}$ or $\frac{2}{13}$

FUNCTION

Definition: A relationship between two quantities (x and y) so that there is only one value of y for any value of x. x is called the independent variable and y is the dependent variable. $y = f(x)$ is a notation for a function where f stands for the rule to use on any x-value to obtain a y-value. Two variables can be related in some way without being functions. They are relations. A function is a special relation.

Symbol: f

Examples:

1) If 1 pound of apples costs \$0.95 and if the total price of the apples depends on of how many pounds one buys, then $y = 0.95x$. y is the dependent variable (the total price) and x is the independent variable (the amount we buy).

2) $y = x$ is called the identity function.

3) $y = x^2$ is a function, because for any value of x there is only one value of y. $y^2 = x$ is not a function, because if x is 4, for example, then y can be either positive 2 or negative 2. This is a relation only.

Practice:

Which of the following equations are functions?

a) $y = 2x + 3$

b) $y = x^3$

c) $x^2 + y^2 = 9$

GEOMETRY

Definition: The word means measurement of the earth. It involves the study of the properties of shapes that are two-dimensional (plane geometry) and those that are three-dimensional (solid geometry). See also AREA, PERIMETER, and COORDINATE GEOMETRY.

GRAM

Definition: Measuring unit for WEIGHT (MASS) in the METRIC SYSTEM. There are about 28 grams in one ounce.

Abbreviation: g

Examples:

    1) 1000 g = 1 kg (kilogram) (= 2.2 lbs)

    2) 424 g = 1 lb

GRAPH

Definition: A drawing that shows the relationship between numbers or quantities. Graphs are usually drawn with COORDINATE AXES at right (90°) angles.

Examples:

    1) The graph of $y = x + 2$ is a straight line.

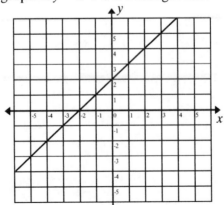

2) The graph of $y = x^2$ is a parabola.

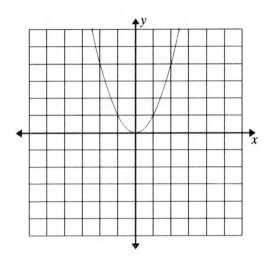

3) See BAR GRAPH.

4) See CIRCLE GRAPH.

GRAPHING

Definition: Plotting ORDERED PAIRS to visualize the location of points or mathematical relationships such as lines or other curves.

Examples:

1) The graph of the points $A(2,3)$, $B(0,4)$, and $C(-4,0)$ looks like this:

Point	X-COORDINATE	Y-COORDINATE
A	2	3
B	0	4
C	-4	0

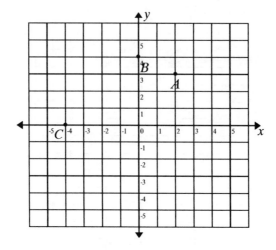

2) The graph of the line $x + y = 4$ looks like this:
    3 points that satisfy the equation $x + y = 4$ are:
    $A = (1,3)$, $B = (2,2)$, and $C = (3,1)$, for example. The
    points are plotted and connected with a straight line.

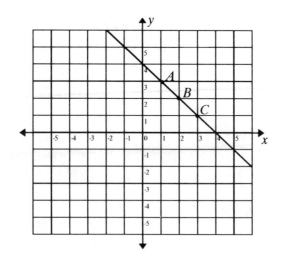

3) The graph of the line $y = 2x + 3$ looks like this:
3 points that satisfy the equation $y = 2x + 3$ are,
for example:

x	y	
0	3	(0,3)
1	5	(1,5)
-1	1	(-1,1)

The points are plotted and connected with a straight
line.

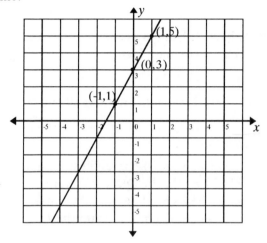

Practice:

Select and plot three points on the line $x + y = 5$.

GREATER THAN

Definition: A comparison of two numbers. On the NUMBER
LINE, the number to the right is the larger (greater) number.

Symbol: > ("is greater than")

Examples:

1) Compare 2 and 6. $6 > 2$ (6 is greater than 2.)

2) 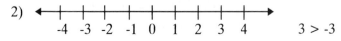 $3 > -3$

111

Practice:

> Show with symbols and on a number line that 2 is a larger number than 0.

GREATEST COMMON FACTOR (GCF)

Definition: The largest number that will divide each of a group of numbers evenly, that is without having a remainder. See also FACTOR.

Example:

> 16 and 24 have 2, 4, and 8 as common factors.
> 8 is the greatest common factor.

Practice:

> Find the greatest common factor of 20 and 50.

GROUPING SYMBOLS

Definition: SYMBOLS, such as parentheses, that indicate numbers and VARIABLES that belong together. In arithmetic, what is inside the parentheses must be simplified first. The different symbols have the same function as parentheses.

Symbols: { } (braces)
         [ ] (brackets)
         ( ) (parentheses)
         — (fraction bars)

Examples:

1) Simplify: $10 - \{4 - 2[1 - 2(2 - 3) - 2]\}$
Simplify inside ( ) first.
$$10 - \{4 - 2[1 - 2(-1) - 2]\}$$
Simplify inside [ ].
$$10 - \{4 - 2[1 + 2 - 2]\} = 10 - \{4 - 2[1]\}$$
Simplify inside { } and replace { } with ( ).
$$10 - (4 - 2) = 10 - (2)$$
$$10 - 2 = 8$$

2) Simplify: $\qquad\qquad 5x - 2[x - 3(x + 2)]$
   Multiply -3 by $(x + 2)$ $\qquad 5x - 2[x - 3x - 6]$
   Simplify inside $[\ ]$ $\qquad\quad 5x - 2[-2x - 6]$
   Multiply -2 by $(-2x - 6)$ $\quad 5x + 4x + 12$
   $\qquad\qquad\qquad\qquad\qquad\quad 9x + 12$

3) Simplify: $\dfrac{10 - 4(3 - 2)}{5 - 3} = \dfrac{10 - 4}{2} = \dfrac{6}{2} = 3$

   The numerator and the denominator are simplified separately.

Practice:

Simplify: $12 - \{20 - [7 + (10 - 8)]\}$

HECTO

Definition: A Latin PREFIX in the METRIC SYSTEM standing for 100.

Symbol: h

Examples:

1) 1 hectogram = 100 grams (1hg = 100g)

2) 1 liter = 0.01 hectoliter (1l = 0.01 hl)

Practice:

How many hectograms are there in 10 grams?

HEIGHT

The length of a line segment going from a VERTEX (corner) perpendicular to the base of a geometric figure. It is the same as the ALTITUDE.

Heptagon

Definition: A POLYGON (many-sided plane figure) with seven sides.

Example:

Hexagon

Definition: A POLYGON (many-sided plane figure) with six sides. All sides of a regular hexagon are equal.

Example:

Horizontal Line

Definition: A line that is parallel with the horizon or the ground.

Hypotenuse

Definition: The largest side in a right (90°) triangle. It is across from the right angle.

See also the PYTHAGOREAN THEOREM.

Example:

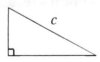

Side *c* is the hypotenuse.

IDENTITY ELEMENTS

Definition: When 0 is added to a number, the number does not change. When a number is multiplied by 1, the number does not change. 0 is called the identity element for addition; 1 is called the identity element for multiplication.

Examples:

1) $5 + 0 = 5$

2) $5 \times 1 = 5$

IMAGINARY NUMBERS

Definition: Numbers that cannot be pictured on the NUMBER LINE; they are not REAL numbers. All SQUARE ROOTS of negative numbers are imaginary numbers, because the square of two numbers cannot be negative.

Example:

$\sqrt{-4}$ is imaginary, because $(2)^2$ and $(-2)^2$ both equal $+4$.

IMPROPER FRACTION

Definition: A fraction in which the NUMERATOR is larger than the DENOMINATOR.

Example:

$$\frac{15}{7}$$

INCREASE

Definition: To make larger by adding.

Example:

To increase 2 by 5, add $2 + 5$.

INDEPENDENT VARIABLE

Definition: If two numbers are related by some kind of rule, one of the numbers can be chosen and the other one has to be calculated using the rule. The VARIABLE that can be chosen is the independent variable; the one that has to be calculated is the dependent variable. The independent variable is the first number of an ORDERED PAIR and is usually called the x-variable.

Examples:

1) If apples cost 99 cents per pound, the price you have to pay for a purchase, y depends on how many pounds you buy. The number of pounds, x, is the independent variable.
   $y = 99x$

2) In the equation $y = mx + b$, x is the independent variable and y is the dependent variable.

INDETERMINATE EXPRESSION

Definition: An expression that has no quantitative meaning. See also UNDEFINED.

Example:

$0 \div 0$ is not possible to determine, because it can be any number. If $0 \div 0 = a$, then $0 \times a = 0$ and a can be any number, because $0 \times b$ is also $= 0$.

INDEX OF ROOTS

Definition: A number written as a superscript to the left of the $\sqrt{}$ of a ROOT SYMBOL. The nth root of a real number such as for example 10, $\sqrt[n]{10}$, has the index n. A square root has the index 2, but it is not written out.

Examples:

1) In $\sqrt{4}$, the index is 2 (square means power of 2).

2) In $\sqrt[3]{8}$, the index is 3.

Practice:

Find the index in the following roots

a) $\sqrt[5]{5}$

b) $\sqrt[9]{45}$

c) $\sqrt{49}$

INEQUALITIES

Definition: A statement that two expressions are not equal.

Symbols: $<$ (less than)
$>$ (greater than)
$\leq$ (less than or equal to)
$\geq$ (greater than or equal to)

Examples:

1) $2 < 3$ This is read as "two is less than three."

2) $3x + 4 \geq 2x + 9$ Note, this inequality is only true for values of x greater than or equal to 5 (see below).

Practice:

Write in symbols "five is greater than two."

Operations:

Addition and subtraction: You may add any number to, or subtract it from, both sides of an inequality and the result will still be an inequality.

Examples:

1) $\begin{array}{r} 2 < 3 \\ +2 \ +2 \\ \hline 4 < 5 \end{array}$

2) $\begin{array}{r} 3x + 4 \geq 2x + 9 \\ -4 \qquad\quad -4 \\ \hline 3x \qquad \geq 2x + 5 \\ -2x \qquad -2x \\ \hline x \quad \geq \qquad 5 \\ x \geq 5 \end{array}$

Practice:

Add 4 to the inequality $2 < 9$.

Multiplication and Division: You may multiply or divide both sides by any positive number.

Examples:

1) $\begin{array}{r} -1 < 2 \\ \times 4 \ \times 4 \\ \hline -4 < 8 \end{array}$

2) $3x > 15$

$\dfrac{3x}{3} > \dfrac{15}{3}$

$x > 5$

Practice:

Multiply the inequality $3 < 5$ by 4.

If you multiply or divide both sides of an inequality by a negative number, reverse the direction of the inequality sign.

Examples:

1) $\qquad -2 < 5$

$-2(-1) \ ? \ 5(-1)$

$2 > -5$

2) $-4x > 12$

$$\frac{-4x}{-4} \, ? \, \frac{12}{-4}$$

$$x < -3$$

Practice:

Multiply the inequality $3 < 5$ by -4.

INSCRIBED

Angle:

Definition: An angle inside a circle with its VERTEX on the circle. Its sides are CHORDS.

Example:

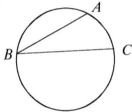

Figure:

Definition: A polygon inside a circle with all its VERTICES on the circle.

Example:

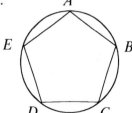

INTEGERS

Definition: The set of the counting numbers, zero, and the opposite (negative) of the counting numbers.
In symbols: $\{..., -3, -2, -1, 0, 1, 2, 3, ...\}$

Example:

–5, 0, and 7 are integers.

Operations:

Addition of two integers:
1. When the signs are alike, add the ABSOLUTE VALUES (symbol | |). The sign of the sum is the sign of the numbers added.
2. When the signs are different, find the difference between the absolute values. The sign of the answer is the sign of the number with the largest absolute value.

Examples:

1) $+2 + (+5) = 7$ $\qquad |+2| = 2 \qquad |+5| = 5$
(Keep the common + sign.)

2) $-2 + (-3) = -5$ $\qquad |-2| = 2 \qquad |-3| = 3$
(Keep the common – sign.)

3) $-4 + 5 = 1$ $\qquad |-4| = 4 \quad |5| = 5 \quad |5| > |-4|$
(Keep the + sign.)

4) $4 + (-5) = -1$ $\quad |4| = 4 \qquad |-5| = 5 \quad |-5| > |4|$
(Keep the – sign.)

Practice: Add

  a) $-1 + (-6)$

  b) $-9 + 7$

Subtraction: To subtract a number, change the subtraction to addition, then change the sign of the second number. Follow the rules for addition.

Examples:

1) $4 - 5 = 4 - (+5) = 4 + (-5) = -1$

2) $-3 - 7 = -3 - (+7) = -3 + (-7) = -10$

3) $5 - (-6) = 5 + 6 = 11$

4) $-7 - (-3) = -7 + 3 = -4$

Practice: Subtract:

a) $-8 - 4$

b) $-8 - (-4)$

Multiplication:

Step 1. Multiply the absolute values of the two numbers.

Step 2. (a) If the signs are the same, the sign of the product (answer) is positive.

(b) If the signs are different, the sign of the product is negative.

Examples:

1) $-2(-5) = 10$

2) $2(-5) = -10$

Practice: Multiply

a) $-4(9)$

b $-4(-9)$

Multiplication of two or more signed numbers: An even number of negative signs gives a positive answer. An odd number of negative signs gives a negative answer.

Examples:

1) $(-1)(-2)(-3)(-4) = +24 = 24;$
   4 minus signs; answer is +

2) $(-2)(-3)(-5) = -30;$ 3 minus signs; answer is –.

Practice: Multiply:

   a) 4(−6)(10)

   b) −4(−6)(10)

Division:

Step 1. Divide the absolute values of the two numbers.

Step 2. (a) If the signs are the same, the sign of the quotient (answer) is plus.

        (b) If the signs are different, the sign of the quotient is minus.

Examples:

   1) $(-15) \div (-3) = 5$

   2) $(-15) \div 3 = -5$

   3) $15 \div (-3) = -5$

Practice:

   Divide

   a) $45 \div (-5)$

   b) $-45 \div (-5)$

Powers:

If a negative number is raised to an even-numbered power (the exponent is even), the result is a positive number.

If a negative number is raised to an odd-numbered power, the result is a negative number.

Examples:

   1) $(-2)^4 = 16$; 4 is even

   2) $(-3)^3 = -27$; 3 is odd

   3) $-(-5)^2 = -(25) = -25$ (Note, the first minus sign does *not* have anything to do with the power!)

Practice:

Evaluate (find the answer):

a) $-(-2)^2$

b) $(-2)^3$

INTERCEPTS

Definition: The points in a graph where a line crosses the axes. The x-intercept has 0 as the y-coordinate and the y-intercept has 0 as the x-coordinate.

Examples:

1)

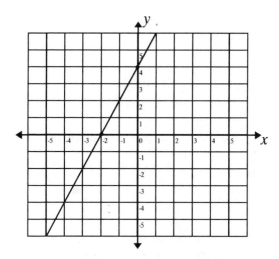

The x-intercept is -2. The y-intercept is 4.

2) The line $x + y = 2$ has 2 as the x-intercept and 2 as the y-intercept, because $x + 0 = 2$ and $0 + y = 2$.

3) The y-intercept of the line $y = mx + b$ is b.
$(y = m(0) + b)$

The x-intercept of the line $y = mx + b$ is $-\dfrac{b}{m}$.
$(0 = mx + b)$

Practice:

Find the x- and the y-intercepts of the line $y = x + 3$.

INTEREST

Definition: The cost of a loan, or money earned for lending a person or a bank money (such as in a savings account). The money borrowed or lent out is called the principal. Interest can be simple or compound.

Formulas:

Simple Interest: $I = Prt$
I = interest
P = principal (the money borrowed or loaned)
r = rate (the percent)
t = time

Compound Interest: $A = P(1 + r)^t$ and $I = A - P$
A is the accumulated principal (principal + interest at a given time).
P = principal (the money borrowed or loaned)
r = rate (the percent)
t = time
I = interest

Examples:

1) For $1000 borrowed for 2 years at a rate of 8% the simple interest is: $1000 \times 8\% \times 2 = \$160$.

2) For $1000 borrowed for 2 years at a rate of 8% compounded monthly, the interest is
$$A - P = \$1000(1 + 8\%/12)^{24} - \$1000$$
$$= \$1000(1.0066...)^{24} - \$1000$$
$$= \$1172.70 - \$1000$$
$$= \$172.70$$

(Calculator answers might vary.)

3) $5000 invested at 3% for 2 months, yields a simple interest of
$5000 \times 3\% \times 2 \div 12 = \$25.00$

4) $5000 invested at 3% for 2 months compounded daily, yields a compound interest of
$\$5000(1 + 3\%/365)^{2 \times 365 \div 12} - \$5000 =$
$\$5000(1.0000822)^{60.83} - \$5000 =$
$\$5025.10 - \$5000 = \$25.10$

Practice: Find

a) The simple interest if $4000 is invested at 2% for 10 years.

b) The interest if the money in practice problem *a* is compounded every month.

INTERIOR

Definition: The inside of a geometric figure.

Example:

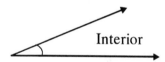

Interior

INTERSECTION

Definition: The common points of geometric figures.

Example:

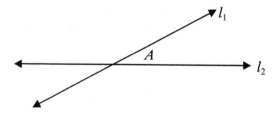

A is the point of intersection of lines l_1 and l_2.

INVERSE

Definition: Two numbers that give 0 as the answer when they are added (additive inverses) or two numbers that give 1 as the answer when they are multiplied (multiplicative inverses). 0 is the IDENTITY ELEMENT for addition and 1 is the IDENTITY ELEMENT for multiplication. The additive inverse is also called the OPPOSITE and the multiplicative inverse is also called the RECIPROCAL.

Examples:

1) $2 + (-2) = 0$ Additive inverses (opposites)

2) $2\left(\dfrac{1}{2}\right) = 1$ Multiplicative inverses. Note, that 2 can be written as $\dfrac{2}{1}$ and $\dfrac{2}{1} \times \dfrac{1}{2} = 1$

3) $\dfrac{2}{3} \times \dfrac{3}{2} = 1$

4) $\left(-\dfrac{3}{4}\right)\left(-\dfrac{4}{3}\right) = 1$

Practice:

a) Add the additive inverse of -4

b) What is the multiplicative inverse of -4?

INVERSE OPERATIONS

Definition: Operations that cancel each other out if the numbers are the same. The following sets of operations cancel each other out:

Addition/subtraction
Multiplication/division
Raising to a power/taking the root

Examples:

1) $5 + 2 - 2 = 5$

2) $3 \times 4 \div 4 = 3$

3) $(\sqrt{5})^2 = 5$

INVERT

Definition: To turn over a fraction; to write its RECIPROCAL (also called the INVERSE.)

Formula: Invert $\dfrac{a}{b}$ to get $\dfrac{b}{a}$; a and b cannot equal 0

Examples:

1) Invert $\dfrac{3}{4}$ to get $\dfrac{4}{3}$.

2) Invert $-\dfrac{2}{5}$ to get $-\dfrac{5}{2}$.

3) Invert 6 to get $\dfrac{1}{6}$.

Practice: Invert

a) $\dfrac{1}{5}$

b) -7

IRRATIONAL NUMBERS

Definition: A number that cannot be written as a division of two INTEGERS (that is, as a fraction). Its representation is a nonterminating, nonrepeating DECIMAL. Compare with RATIONAL NUMBERS.

Example:

1) $\sqrt{2} \approx 1.414213...$

2) $\pi \approx 3.141592...$

Practice:

Which of the following is an irrational number?

a) 0.12

b) $\sqrt{9}$

c) 2.6457513...

ISOSCELES TRIANGLE

Definition: A triangle with two equal sides.

Example:

In triangle *ABC*, the sides *a* and *b* are equal. The angles *A* and *B* are also equal.

KILO

Definition: A Latin PREFIX in the METRIC SYSTEM standing for 1000.

Symbol: k

Examples:

1) 1 kilogram = 1000 grams (1 kg = 1000 g)

2) 1 meter = 0.001 kilometer (1 m = 0.001 km)

Practice:

How many kilometers are there in 100 meters?

Laws

See PROPERTIES, Appendix 3 on page 23.

Least (Or Lowest) Common Denominator (LCD)

Definition: The expression for the smallest number that is a MULTIPLE of the DENOMINATORS (bottom numbers) for two or more fractions. See also LCM.

Examples:

1) $\frac{1}{4}$ and $\frac{1}{6}$ have 12, 24, 36, ... as common denominators. 12 is the LCD.

2) $\frac{1}{(x+1)^2}, \frac{1}{(x+1)(x-1)},$ and $\frac{1}{(x-1)^2}$ have $(x + 1)^2(x - 1)^2$ as the LCD.

Practice:

Find the least common denominator of $\frac{1}{12}$ and $\frac{1}{18}$.

Least Common Multiple (LCM)

Definition: The smallest number that is a MULTIPLE of two or more numbers.

Examples:

1) Find the LCM of 15 and 12.
   The multiples of 15 are:
       15, 30, 45, 60, 75, 90, 105, 120, ...
   The multiples of 12 are:
       12, 24, 36, 48, 60, 72, 84, 96, 108, 120, ...
   Common multiples are 60, 120, 180, 240, ...
   60 is the least (smallest) common multiple (LCM).

Alternate method:

Factor the numbers as far as possible (that is, into PRIME factors).

$15 = 3 \times 5$ and $12 = 4 \times 3 = 2^2 \times 3$

The factors are 2, 3, and 5, but 2 occurs twice in the number 12.

Therefore, the LCM is $2 \times 2 \times 3 \times 5 = 60$

2) Find the LCM of a, $9a$, and $3a^2$

The prime factors are 3 and a. 2 factors of each are needed:

$9 = 3 \times 3 = 3^2$

$a^2 = a \times a$

The LCM is $3^2 a^2 = 9a^2$

3) Find the LCM of $x^2 + 2x$ and $x^2 - 4$.

FACTOR both expressions:

$x^2 + 2x = x(x + 2)$

$x^2 - 4 = (x + 2)(x - 2)$

The factors are x, $x + 2$, and $x - 2$. One factor of each is needed.

The LCM is $x(x + 2)(x - 2)$.

Practice:

Find the LCM of 16 and 18.

LEGS

Definition: The two shorter sides in a right triangle.

Example:

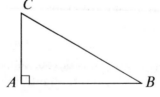

$\overline{AB}$ and $\overline{AC}$ are the legs.

$\overline{BC}$ is the HYPOTENUSE.

LENGTH

Definition: The total distance along a line. The basic unit of length in the METRIC SYSTEM is the meter. One meter is a little longer a yard.

Examples:

1) 1 meter = 100 centimeters (1 m = 100 cm)

2) In a rectangle, the longest side is called the length.

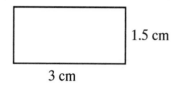

3 cm

The length is 3 cm.

LESS THAN

Definition: A number that is smaller than another number. It can always be found to the left of another number on the NUMBER LINE.

Symbol: < ("is less than")

Examples:

1) 2 < 6 (2 is less than 6).

2) Write −5 is less than 0 in symbols. −5 < 0

Practice:

Write −10 is smaller than −6 in symbols.

LIKE TERMS

Definition: TERMS in which both VARIABLES and EXPONENTS match.

Example:

5*x* and 3*x* are like terms. 5*x* and $3x^2$ are not like terms.

Practice:

Mark the like terms: $2ax^2$, a^2x, $7ax^2$, $3a^2x^2$

LINE

Definition: An infinite collection of points. A line has direction but neither a beginning nor an end.

Examples:

1) Line

2) A HORIZONTAL LINE

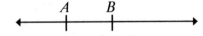

LINE SEGMENT

Definition: Part of a line with a beginning and an end.

Symbol: $^-$ (a bar above the points defining the beginning and end of the line segment)

Example:

$\overline{AB}$ is a line segment. $\overleftrightarrow{AB}$ is a line.

AB is the length of the line segment.

LINEAR EQUATION

Definition: An equation in which the variables are raised to the first power. Note that the first power is never written out.

For example, x^1 is written as x. The GRAPH of a linear equation is a straight line.

See also SOLVING LINEAR EQUATIONS.

Examples:

1) $x + 2 = 5$

2) $y = 3x - 2$

LITER

Definition: A unit of VOLUME in the METRIC SYSTEM. One liter is about the same as one quart.

Abbreviation: l

Example:

1) 1 liter = 100 centiliters (1 l = 100 cl)

2) 1 cl = 0.01 l

Practice:

How many centiliters are there in 2.5 l?

LONG DIVISION

Definition: An ALGORITHM (procedure) to perform division with numbers or POLYNOMIALS. Long division is not very common any more because we use calculators, but for further study of mathematics (precalculus and calculus), it is essential. The technique used in algebra is the same as the one used in arithmetic.

To divide for example 123 by 3, the problem is set up the following way:

$3\overline{)123}$ 3 does not go into 1 but into 12. It goes 4 times.

$\dfrac{4}{3\overline{)123}}$ Write 4 above the 2 in 12.
   4 times 3 is 12.

$\dfrac{4}{3\overline{)123}}$
$-12\downarrow$ Write −12 below 12 and subtract.
   Carry down 3.
   3   3 goes into 3 once.

$\dfrac{41}{3\overline{)123}}$ Write 1 next to 4.
-12
$\overline{3}$
-3
$\overline{0}$ remainder

The answer (quotient) is 41.

Examples:

1) $259 \div 13$

$\dfrac{19\text{R}12}{13\overline{)259}}$
$-13\downarrow$
$\overline{129}$
-117
$\overline{12}$

12 is the remainder and can be written as R12 or as a fraction where 12 is the numerator and 13 (the divisor) is the denominator.

$\dfrac{19.923...}{13\overline{)259}}$
-13
$\overline{129}$
-117
$\overline{120}$ Add a 0 and
-117 put a decimal
$\overline{30}$ point in the
-26 quotient.
$\overline{40}$
-39
$\overline{1}$

Round the answer to a convenient number of decimals. It could be 20, 19.9, or 19.92.

2) $x^2 + 5x - 3 \div (x + 1)$

$$x + 1 \overline{) \begin{array}{l} x + 4 \frac{-7}{x+1} \\ x^2 + 5x - 3 \end{array}}$$ x goes into x^2 x times.

$\underline{-x^2 - x}$ Multiply $x + 1$ by x and subtract.

    $4x - 3$ Carry down -3. x goes into $4x$ 4 times.

   $\underline{-4x - 4}$ Multiply $x + 1$ by 4 and subtract.

    -7

The remainder is -7 and is written as a fraction $\frac{-7}{x+1}$.

Practice:

  a) Divide 364 by 7 using long division.

  b) Divide $\dfrac{x^2 + 5x + 6}{x + 2}$ using long division.

LOWEST TERMS

Definition: A fraction where neither the NUMERATOR (top number) nor the DENOMINATOR (bottom number) of a fraction have FACTORS that are the same. See also FRACTIONS.

Example:

  1) $\dfrac{5}{8}$

  2) $\dfrac{a + b}{a - b}$

     Note that neither *a* nor *b* is a factor. They are terms. (Factors are separated by a multiplication sign. Terms are separated by plus or minus signs.)

MAGNITUDE

Definition: The value of a number without regard to sign. See also ABSOLUTE VALUE.

Examples:

1) The magnitude of 5 is 5.

2) The magnitude of −10 is 10.

Practice:

What is the magnitude of −7?

MASS

Definition: A measure of the quantity of matter in an object. Mass is used interchangeably with weight in everyday language.

Example:

The mass of 1 liter of water is 1 kilogram.

MEAN

Definition: The numerical AVERAGE of data. The mean is obtained by adding all the data and dividing by the number of data items.

Symbol: $\bar{x}$ (read as "x bar").

Example:

The mean of 6, 9, 4, and 5 is $\dfrac{6+9+4+5}{4} = \dfrac{24}{4} = 6$.

$\bar{x} = 6$

Practice:

Find the mean of 1, 2, 3, 3, 4, and 5.

MEASUREMENTS

Definition: To determine properties (such as weight and length) and compare them with a given standard or unit. See CUSTOMARY SYSTEM and METRIC SYSTEM.

MEDIAN

In statistics:

Definition: The middle number is a set of numbers arranged in order.

Symbol: $\tilde{x}$ (read as "x tilde").

Examples:

1) If the set of numbers is 1, 2, 3, 4, 5, the median is 3.
$$\tilde{x} = 3$$

2) If the set of numbers is 1, 2, 3, 4, the median is
$$\frac{2+3}{2} = \frac{5}{2} = 2.5.$$
$$\tilde{x} = 2.5$$

Practice:

Find the median of 1, 2, 3, 3, 4, 5.

In geometry:

Definition: A line segment from one vertex (corner) to the midpoint of the opposite side in a triangle.

Example:

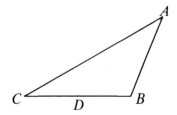

$\overline{AD}$ is the median when $CD = DB$.

Meter

Definition: A unit of length in the METRIC SYSTEM. It is slightly more than 1 yard (39.37 inches).

Abbreviation: m

Examples:

    1) 100 centimeters = 1 meter (100 cm = 1 m)

    2) 1 cm = 0.01 m

Practice:

    How many centimeters are there in 1.5 meters?

Metric System

Definition: This system was developed in France and is used extensively in Europe and in many parts of the world. Scientists everywhere use this system. It is built on POWERS OF 10 and to convert between different units one has only to multiply or divide by 10, 100, 1000, etc. (See also PLACE VALUE.)

The basic units are meter, gram, and liter. Metric measuring units have Latin prefixes, e.g. kilometer, hectogram, milliliter).

Length is measured in meters. One meter is approximately equal to one yard (39.37 inches).

Mass (weight) is measured in grams, which is about 0.0353 ounces. There are 28 grams in one ounce. 1000 grams (1 kilogram) is about 2 pounds (2.2 lbs).

Volume is measured in liters, where 1 liter is roughly 1 quart (1.0567 quarts).

Examples:

    1) He is nearly 2 meters tall.

    2) Lynn bought 100 grams of candy.

    3) I need 1 liter of milk to bake bread.

The prefixes are:

    kilo (k) = thousand
    hecto (h) = hundred
    deka (da) = ten
    deci (d) = tenth
    centi (c) = hundredth
    milli (m) = thousandth

Examples:

1) 1 kilometer = 10 hectometer

2) 1 hectometer = 10 decameter

3) 1 dekameter = 10 meter and so on

The measuring units for length, mass, and volume can all be demonstrated in columns with the basic units as meter, gram, and liter.

kilo	hecto	deka	basic unit	deci	centi	milli

Conversions:

Within the metric system:

Length: The basic unit is meter, which is abbreviated m.

    km | hm | dam | m | dm | cm | mm

Each column contains one digit. There are 10 mm in 1 cm, 10 cm in 1 dm, 10 dm in 1 m, 10 m in 1 dam, 10 dam in 1 hm, and 10 hm in 1 km. Convert from one unit to another by placing the ones digit (the number before the decimal point) below the name of the measuring unit. Mark the decimal point.

Examples:

1) To determine how many meters there are in one kilometer, move the decimal point three places to the right (to get to the meter). Insert zeros when needed. (In this case the kilometer is considered as the measuring unit.)

km	hm	dam	m	dm	cm	mm
1.	0	0	0			

km	hm	dam	m	dm	cm	mm
1	0	0	0.			

1 km = 1000 m

2) To convert 350 millimeters to meters, move the decimal point three places to the left (to the meter). 0 is the digit in the ones place. The measuring unit is mm.

km	hm	dam	m	dm	cm	mm
				3	5	0.

350 mm = 0.350 m

Practice: Convert:

a) 15 decimeters to meters.

b) 0.4 meters to centimeters.

Weight (mass): The basic unit is gram, which is abbreviated g.

kg	hg	dag	g	dg	cg	mg

Examples:

1) To change 0.5 kilograms to grams, move the decimal point three places to the right.

kg	hg	dag	g	dg	cg	mg
.	5	0	0			

0.5 kg = 500 g

2) To convert 4300 milligrams to hectograms, move the decimal point five places to the left (insert 0 in the empty column).

kg	hg	dag	g	dg	cg	mg
			4	3	0	0.

kg	hg	dag	g	dg	cg	mg
.		0	4	3	0	0

4300 mg = 0.043 hg

Practice: Convert:

 a) 500 grams to kilograms.

 b) 1 hectogram to grams.

Volume (liquid): The basic unit is liter, which is abbreviated l.

  kl │ hl │ dal │ l │ dl │ cl │ ml

Examples:

 1) To change 5.4 liters to deciliters, move the decimal point one place to the right.

  kl │ hl │ dal │ l │ dl │ cl │ ml

        5. 4

  5.4 l = 54 dl

 2) To convert 375 milliliters to centiliters, move the decimal point one place to the left.

  kl │ hl │ dal │ l │ dl │ cl │ ml

          3   7   5.

  375 ml = 37.5 cl

Practice: Convert:

 a) 0.6 dekaliters to deciliters.

 b) 750 ml to l.

Volume (solid): The metric system uses a three-dimensional unit, the cubic meter as the basic unit for solid volume. A box has three dimensions: length, width, and height.

  m^3 │ dm^3 │ cm^3 │ mm^3

$1 \ dm^3 = 1 \ dm \times 1 \ dm \times 1 \ dm = 10 \ cm \times 10 \ cm \times 10 \ cm = 1000 \ cm^3$, so there is room for 3 digits in each column.

Examples:

 1) To convert 0.006 cubic meters to cubic centimeters, move the decimal point $3 \times 2 = 6$ places to the right.

  m^3 │ dm^3 │ cm^3 │ mm^3

  0.006 000

  $0.006 \ m^3 = 6000 \ cm^3$

2) To change 25,000 cubic decimeters to cubic meters, move the decimal point $3 \times 1 = 3$ places to the left.

m³	dm³	cm³	mm³
25	000.		

$25,000 \text{ dm}^3 = 25 \text{ m}^3$

Practice: Convert:

a) 0.005 cubic meters to cubic centimeters.

b) 1.5 cm³ to mm³.

Area: Area is a surface. It is measured in square units. A rectangle, for example, has an area of length × width. The most common metric unit for area is the square meter (m²). Other units are: square decimeter (dm²), square centimeter (cm²), and square millimeter (mm²).

km²	hm²	dam²	m²	dm²	cm²	mm²

$10 \text{ cm} \times 10 \text{ cm} = 100 \text{ cm}^2 = 1 \text{ dm} \times 1 \text{ dm} = 1 \text{ dm}^2$

Here there is room for 2 digits in each column.

There are 100 cm² in 1 dm² and 100 dm² in 1 m².

There are 10,000 cm² in 1 m².

Examples:

1) To convert 5000 square centimeters to square meters, move the decimal point $2 \times 2 = 4$ places to the left.

km²	hm²	dam²	m²	dm²	cm²	mm²
			50	00.		

$5000 \text{ cm}^2 = 0.5 \text{ m}^2$

2) To change 4 square kilometers to square meters, move the decimal point $3 \times 2 = 6$ places to the right.

km²	hm²	dam²	m²	dm²	cm²	mm²
4.	00	00	00			

$4 \text{ km}^2 = 4,000,000 \text{ m}^2$

Practice:

Convert 2 dm² to cm².

Metric/customary conversions:

Conversion factors: (The conversion factors are approximate, which is denoted with ≈.)

Length: 2.54 cm ≈ 1 inch
Mass: 1 kg ≈ 2.2 lb
            454 g ≈ 1 lb
Volume: 1 l ≈ 1 quart

Example:

1)   15 cm ≈ 15 ÷ 2.54 inches = 5.9 inches

2)   25 in ≈ 25 × 2.54 cm = 63.5 cm

3)   50 kg ≈ 50 × 2.2 lb. = 110 lb.

4)   130 lb. ≈ 130 ÷ 2.2 kg = 59 kg

5)   1 cup = ¼ quart ≈ ¼ l = 0.25 l = 2.5 dl

Practice: Convert:

a)   100 meters to yards.

b)   100 grams to ounces. (How many ounces are there in one pound?)

MIDPOINT

Definition: A point that divides a LINE SEGMENT into two equal parts.

Example:

$$A \qquad\qquad B \qquad\qquad C$$

B is the midpoint between *A* and *C*, provided that
$AB = BC$

MIXED NUMBER

Definition: A number consisting of a whole number together with a fraction. See FRACTIONS.

Example:

$$4\frac{3}{4}$$

MIXTURE PROBLEMS

Definition: Problems with mixtures such as of liquids or of coins of different denominations.

Template (form):

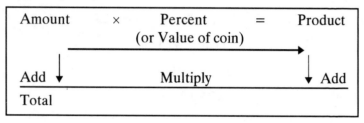

Examples:

1) How many gallons of a 60% alcohol solution should be added to 30 gallons of a 10% alcohol solution to make a 20% alcohol solution?

    Set up the problem according to the template:

Amount		Percent		Product
x gal	×	60%	=	x (60%)
30 gal	×	10%	=	30(10%)
$(x + 30)$ gal	×	20%	=	$(x + 30)$ 20%

The entries in the product column are added and are equal to the product in the total row:

$$x\,(60\%) + 30(10\%) = (x + 30)(20\%)$$
$$60x + 30(10) = 20(x + 30)$$

(multiply by 100 to eliminate %)

$$60x + 300 = 20x + 600$$
$$40x = 300$$
$$x = 7.5$$

Answer: 7.5 gallons

2) Liz has 20 coins, all nickels and dimes. The total value of the coins is $1.35. Use the template to determine how many of each type coin Liz has.

Amount	Value of coin	Total value
x	5¢	5x ¢
y	10¢	10y ¢
Total $x + y$		5x + 10y ¢

Equations:

$x + y = 20$ Total number of coins = 20
$5x + 10y = 135$ Total value of coins = 135

Multiply the first equation by –5 (to eliminate x):

$$-5x - 5y = -100$$
$$\underline{5x + 10y = \ 135}$$
$$5y = 35$$
$$y = 7$$

Substitute 7 for y in the first equation.

$$x + 7 = 20$$
$$x = 13$$

Answer: There are 13 nickels and 7 dimes.

Practice:

Carl bought 120 stamps at the post office. Some were 60-cent stamps and others were 34 cents. How many of each kind did he buy if the total cost was $ 43.40?

MODE

Definition: The number that occurs most often in a set of numbers.

Examples:

1) In 1, 2, 2, 3, 4, 5, 2 is the mode.

2) In 4, 5, 5, 6, 7, 7, 7, 8, 8, 9, 9, 9, there are two modes: 7 and 9.

Practice:

Find the mode: 6, 9, 8, 8,7, 8, 10, 7.

MONOMIALS

Definition: One term consisting of constants and variables. See also POLYNOMIALS.

Example:

$5x^5y^3$

Operations:

Addition and subtraction: Monomials can be added if they are LIKE TERMS (that is, they have the same variables and exponents). The coefficients are added or subtracted.

Example:

$5x^5y^3 + 7x^5y^3 = 12x^5y^3$

Practice:

Subtract: $8ab - 5ab$

Multiplication: Multiply the coefficients and add the exponents when the bases are the same.

Example:

$(2a^2b)(3ab^3) = 6a^3b^4$

Practice:

Multiply $3xy(4xy^3)$.

Division: Divide the coefficients and subtract the exponents when the bases are the same.

Example:

$25a^5b^3 \div 5ab^2 = 5a^4b$

Practice:

Divide $16x^3y^5$ by $4xy$.

Powers:

Raise each factor to the indicated power.

Example:

$$\left(2x^2y^3\right)^4 = 2^4 x^8 y^{12} = 16x^8 y^{12}$$

Practice:

Raise to the indicated power: $\left(5a^3b\right)^3$

MORE THAN

Definition: The expression means "add the first number to the second." (Note: more than has a different meaning from "greater than," which describes an INEQUALITY.)

Example:

4 more than 2 is 2 + 4.

MOTION (RATE) PROBLEMS

Definition: Problems dealing with distance, rate, and time.

Formula: $d = rt$

Template (form):

	Case I	Case II
Rate		
Time		
Distance		

Examples:

1) Two trains leave the station at the same time going in opposite directions. One train has a speed of 40 miles per hour and the other has a speed of 60 miles per hour. In how many hours will they be 500 miles apart?

Here $r = 40$ for the first train and 60 for the second train. The time is not known, so it is called x. Use the formula to obtain expressions for the distances the two trains have traveled.

	Train 1	Train 2
Rate	40 mph	60 mph
Time	x hrs	x hrs
Distance	$40x$ mi	$60x$ mi
Equation:	$40x + 60x = 500$ (miles)	
	$100x = 500$	
	$x = 5$	

Answer: 5 hours

2) A plane can travel 600 miles per hour with the wind and 450 miles per hour against the wind. Find the speed of the plane in still air and the speed of the wind.

Call the speed of the plane x and the speed of the wind y.

	With the wind	Against the wind
Rate	$x + y$ mph	$x - y$ mph
Time	1 hr	1 hr
Distance	600 mi	450 mi
Equations:	$(x + y)1 = 600$	
	$(x - y)1 = 450$	
	$2x = 1050$	
	$x = 525$	
	$y = 75$	

Answer: The speed of the plane is 525 mph.
The speed of the wind is 75 mph.

Practice:

Kaye can row 24 miles downstream in 3 hours. But when she rows upstream the same distance, it takes 6 hours. Find Kaye's rate in still water and the rate of the current.

MULTIPLE

Definition: When a number is multiplied by 1, 2, 3, ... we get multiples of that number.

Examples:

1) $1 \times 6 = 6$ $2 \times 6 = 12$ $3 \times 6 = 18$
    6, 12, and 18 are multiples of 6.

2) Multiples of 5 are 5, 10, 15, 20, 25, ...

Practice:

List the first six multiples of 8.

MULTIPLICATION

Definition: Multiplication is the same as repeated addition. The answer is called the product.

Example:

$2 \times 3 = 3 + 3$
$4 \times 3 = 3 + 3 + 3 + 3$

MULTIPLICATIVE INVERSE

Definition: A number times its inverse equals one. It is the same as the RECIPROCAL. To find the inverse of a fraction, turn the fraction upside down.

Example:

$\frac{2}{3}$ is the multiplicative inverse of $\frac{3}{2}$.

NATURAL NUMBERS

Definition: The numbers that came naturally to us as young children. It is the same as COUNTING NUMBERS and POSITIVE INTEGERS.

Example:

1, 2, 3, 4, 5, ... are natural numbers.

NEGATIVE EXPONENTS

Definition: See EXPONENT. Negative exponents are changed to positive when the number is inverted (turned upside down).

Formula: $a^{-n} = \dfrac{1}{a^n}$

Examples:

1) $2^{-1} = \dfrac{1}{2}$

2) $\dfrac{1}{3^{-2}} = 3^2 = 9$

3) $\dfrac{a^{-2}}{b^{-3}} = \dfrac{b^3}{a^2}$

Practice:

Write $\dfrac{2^{-1}}{3^{-2}}$ without negative exponents.

NEGATIVE NUMBERS

Definition: Any number with a negative sign preceding it. The rules of operations are the same as those for the INTEGERS.

Examples:

$-2,\ -0.4,\ -\dfrac{3}{5}$

Nonagon

Definition: A polygon (many-sided figure) with nine sides.

Example:

Nonterminating Decimals

Definition: Numbers in which the decimal never ends. These decimal numbers can be REPEATING or not.

Symbol: ...

Examples:

1) 0.12121... is a repeating, nonterminating decimal. It can also be written as $0.\overline{12}$ where the bar goes above the whole repeating group.

2) $\sqrt{2} \approx 1.1412135...$ is a nonrepeating, nonterminating decimal.

Number

Definition: An abstract concept of amount. Symbols for numbers are called NUMERALS. (For a detailed description of numbers, see Appendix 1 on page 19.)

Number Line

Definition: Pictorial representation of numbers.

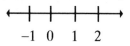

Example:

Show $-2 + 5$ on the number line.

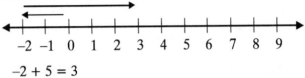

$-2 + 5 = 3$

NUMBER PROBLEMS

Definition: Such problems deal often with consecutive odd or even integers. Another type is straight translations. Consecutive integers (1, 2, 3,...) are one apart. Consecutive even integers (2, 4, 6,...), as well as consecutive odd integers (1, 3, 5, ...), are two apart.

Examples:

1) The sum of three consecutive even integers is 36. Find the integers.

Call the first integer x

First integer	x
Second integer	$x + 2$
Third integer	$x + 4$
Sum	$3x + 6 = 36$
	$x = 10$

First integer $= 10$
Second integer $= 12$
Third integer $= 14$

2) One number is 4 less than twice another number. Their sum is 14. Find the numbers.

Call the numbers x and y.

$x = 2y - 4$

$x + y = 14$

Solve by substitution.

$y = 6 \quad x = 8$

Answer: The numbers are 6 and 8.

Practice:

> The sum of three consecutive integers is 33. Find the numbers.

NUMERAL

Definition: Symbol for a number.

Example:

> 7 is the symbol for the amount seven. Another symbol for seven is VII.

NUMERATION SYSTEMS

Definition: Systems of counting and writing numbers.

Examples:

1) The Egyptian way of writing 10 was ∩. The Roman way was X.
    The Egyptians gave a value to each symbol. | = one and ∩ = ten. The order of the symbols does not matter. For example, ||| ∩ ∩ = ∩ ∩ ||| = 23

2) The Hindu-Arabic numeration system (our system) uses 10 digits and a place value for each.

NUMERATOR

Definition: The top number in a FRACTION.

Example:

> In $\frac{3}{4}$, 3 is the numerator.

NUMERICAL COEFFICIENT

Definition: Same as COEFFICIENT (the number that precedes a variable).

NUMERICAL EQUATION

Definition: A mathematical statement that two NUMERICAL EXPRESSIONS are equal.

Examples:

1) $2 + 3 = 1 + 4$

2) $10 - 5(3 - 1) = 10 - 15 + 5$ (Both sides equal 0.)

NUMERICAL EXPRESSION

Definition: A collection of numbers and operations.

Example:

1) $4(2) - 3$

2) $10 - 2(\sqrt{9} - 3^2)$

OBTUSE ANGLE

Definition: An angle that measures more than 90°. Compare ACUTE ANGLE.

Example:

Angle α is obtuse.

OCTAGON

Definition: A polygon (many-sided figure) with eight sides.

Example:

ODD NUMBERS

Definition: 1, 3, 5, 7, ...

Example:

> The odd numbers between 100 and 110 are 101, 103, 105, 107, and 109.

OPERATION

Definition: The performance of one number on another number. The BASIC OPERATIONS are addition, subtraction, multiplication, and division.

OPPOSITES

Definition: A number with the same ABSOLUTE VALUE as another number but with the opposite sign. The sum of two opposite numbers is 0. Opposite numbers are also called ADDITIVE INVERSES.

Examples:

> 1) The opposites of 2, –5, and 0 are –2, 5, and 0.
>
> 2) 5 + (–5) = 0

Practice:

> Which number is its own opposite?

ORDER OF OPERATIONS

Definition: The operations in arithmetic should be done in the following order:

<u>Step 1.</u> Simplify inside any grouping symbols
  (that is, { }, [ ], ( ), and fraction bars).

<u>Step 2.</u> Simplify in this order:
  (a) Evaluate EXPONENTIAL and RADICAL
    expressions.
  (b) Multiply and divide in order from left to right.
  (c) Add and subtract.

The rules are often memorized as **PEMDAS** (parentheses, exponents, multiplication, division, addition, subtraction.

Examples:

1) $10 - 4[3 - (2 - 5)] =$
    $10 - 4[3 - (-3)] =$
    $10 - 4[3 + 3] =$
    $10 - 4(6) =$
    $10 - 24 = -14$

2) $16 \div 4(2) = 4(2) = 8$ (Follow step 2b.)

3) $(2 + 5)^2 = 7^2 = 49$

4) $\sqrt{9 + 16} = \sqrt{25} = 5$

Practice: Simplify

  a) $15 \div 5(3)$

  b) $\dfrac{5 \times 3^2 + 6}{3 \times 5 + 2}$

ORDERED PAIR

Definition: Two numbers (x, y) which are written in order, first x then y.

Example:

In $(6, 3)$ $x = 6$ and $y = 3$.

ORDINATE

Definition: The second number in an ordered pair. It is also called the *Y*-COORDINATE. Compare ABSCISSA.

Examples:

1) In $(6, 3)$, the ordinate is 3.

2) In a graph, the ordinate is shown as the vertical distance between a point and the *x*-axis.

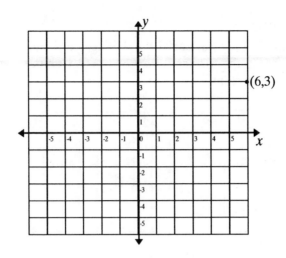

Practice:

What is the ordinate of the point (-5,9)?

ORIGIN

Definition: The point where the COORDINATE AXES intersect. The point (0,0) is the origin.

Example:

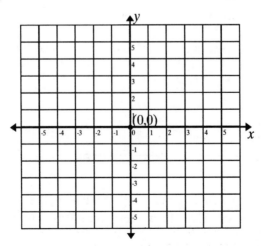

157

PARABOLA

Definition: A special curve that changes direction once. The equation is in the format $y = ax^2 + bx + c$. Compare with LINEAR EQUATIONS.

Example:

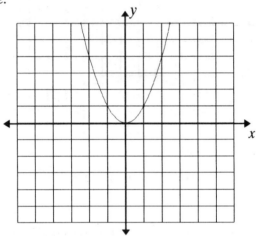

$y = x^2$ (in this case both b and $c = 0$)

PARALLEL LINES

Definition: Lines that do not intersect. These lines have the same SLOPE.

Examples:

1)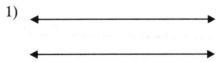

2) For two lines, $y = 2x$ and $y = 2x + 5$, the slope of both lines is 2. Therefore, these are parallel lines.

PARALLELOGRAM

Definition: A quadrilateral (four-sided figure) with both pairs of opposite sides parallel.

Example:

PARENTHESES

Definition: Symbols that keep numbers or expressions together. The order of operations rule directs us to simplify inside parentheses first. The grouping symbols { } (braces), [ ] (brackets), and ( ) (parentheses) are all interchangeable. Computer programs are usually written with ( ) nested within each other— that is, (( )).

Examples:

1) $10 - 2(3 - 1) = 10 - 2(2) = 10 - 4$

2) $5\{2-[5-(3-1)]\}$ could also be written as $5(2-(5-(3-1)))$.

Practice:

Rewrite $50 - 2\{3[2(5 - 4) + 6]\}$ with nested parentheses.

PENTAGON

Definition: A polygon (many-sided figure) with five sides.

Example:

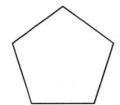

PERCENT

Definition: The word itself means "per hundred." Per means "divided by." In theory, if we are asked to add 5% and 10%, we get 15%. But in reality, 5% usually means 5% *of* something and 10% might mean 10% of something else. If your calculator has a % key, try to add 5% and 10%. Do you get 15%?

Try this: 100 + 10% – 10%. Did you get 100? Or did you get 99?

Mathematically, % means divide by 100, so in the cases above, you should be able to add 5% and 10% and get 15%. However, if the calculator is programmed differently, you might get an answer of 0.055. This is because 5% is registered as 0.05 and 10% as 10% of 0.05, which is 0.10 times 0.05 = 0.005. Add that to 0.05 and the answer is 0.055.

In the second case 10% – 10% should cancel out, but the calculator might be programmed to add

100 + 10% of 100 = 100 + 10, which is 110.

Then it would calculate 110 – 10% of 110 = 110 – 11 = 99.

Conversions:

Percents into decimals: Divide by 100. That is, move the decimal point two places to the left.

Examples:

1) 5% = 5.% = 0.05

2) 0.1% = 0.001

3) 100% = 100.% = 1. = 1

Practice:

Convert 25% to a decimal.

Percents into fractions: Divide by 100.

Examples:

1) $5\% = \dfrac{5}{100} = \dfrac{1}{20}$

2) $100\% = \dfrac{100}{100} = 1$

Practice:

Convert 25% to a fraction.

Numbers into percents: Multiply by 100%.

Examples:

1) $0.002 = 0.002 \times 100\% = 0.2\%$

2) $1.5 = 1.5 \times 100\% = 150\%$

3) $\frac{2}{5} = \frac{2}{5} \times 100\% = \frac{200\%}{5} = 40\%$

4) $\frac{1}{3} = \frac{100\%}{3} = 33\frac{1}{3}\%$

Practice: Convert to percents:

a) 0.125

b) $\frac{1}{8}$

Problem solving:

The word *of* means "times." 15% of 10 means

$15\% \times 10 = 0.15 \times 10 = 1.5$

If a store advertises that an item has been reduced 25% and you can take off an additional 15%, how many percent is the final reduction of the item? Is it 40%?

For simplicity, let's assume that the original price was $100. Because 25% was taken off, that is 25% of 100 = $25. You should now pay $75, but get another 15% discount. That is 15% of $75. Your new reduction is 15% of 75 = $11.25. The total reduction is $25 + $11.25 = $36.25 or 36.25% of the original $100!

Percent problems solved with proportions:

Percent problems can often be rewritten in a simple form: What percent of some number equals another number? We are asked to find one number when the other two are given.

For example:

<u>Type 1</u>	What percent of 50 is 5?
<u>Type 2</u>	10% of what number is 5?
<u>Type 3</u>	10% of 50 is what?

All these problems can be solved by the use of proportions, by arithmetic, and by direct translation into algebra.

Many people use a formula: " percent, 100, is, of " for solving percent problems. Below are some standard types of percent problems solved by this method.

Template (form): $\dfrac{Percent}{100} = \dfrac{is}{of}$

Example: <u>Type 1</u>

What percent of 50 is 5?

$$\frac{N}{100} = \frac{5}{50}$$

Cross-multiply: $50N = 500$

$$\frac{50N}{50} = \frac{500}{50}$$

$$N = 10$$

Answer: 10%

Practice:

Tom solved 20 problems correctly on a 25-question test. What percent was that?

Example: <u>Type 2</u>

10% of what number is 5?

$$\frac{10}{100} = \frac{5}{N}$$

Cross-multiply: $10N = 500$

$$\frac{10N}{10} = \frac{500}{10}$$

$$N = 50$$

Practice:

50% of what number is 3?

Example: <u>Type 3</u>

10% of 50 is what number?

$$\frac{10}{100} = \frac{N}{50}$$

Cross-multiply: $500 = 100N$

$5 = N$

Practice:

What is 30% of 500?

Instead of using equations with a variable, one can solve the same problems using arithmetic, as follows:

<u>Type 1.</u>   Solve by division.

Example:

What percent of 50 is 5?

$$\frac{5}{50} = \frac{1}{10} = \frac{100\%}{10} = 10\%$$

Practice:

Tom solved 20 problems correctly on a 25-question test. What percent was that?

<u>Type 2.</u>   Solve by division.

Example:

10% of what number is 5?

$$\frac{5}{10\%} = \frac{5}{0.10} = \frac{50}{1} = 50$$

Practice:

50% of what number is 3?

<u>Type 3.</u>   Solve by multiplication.

Example:

10% of 50 is what number?

$$0.10 \times 50 = 5 \text{ or } \frac{10}{100} \times 50 = \frac{500}{100} = 5$$

Practice:

What is 30% of 500?

Percent problems solved with algebra:

These problems can also by used by direct translation. Call the unknown number x. Write an equation and solve.

Examples:

1) What percent of 50 is 5?
   $$x \cdot 50 = 5$$
   $$x = \frac{5}{50}$$
   $$x = \frac{1}{10} \text{ or } 10\%$$

2) 10% of what number is 5?
   $$10\%x = 5$$
   $$x = \frac{5}{10\%}$$
   $$x = \frac{5}{0.10}$$
   $$x = 50$$

3) 10% of 50 is what number?
   $$10\% \cdot 50 = x$$
   $$0.10 \cdot 50 = x$$
   $$5 = x$$

Practice: Solve

   a) What percent of 25 is 20?

b) 50% of what number is 3?

c) What is 30% of 500?

Percent added or subtracted:

Many practical percent problems deal with cases in which the percent is either already added or subtracted and you need to find the original base number (the "of" number). Let a stand for any number. To find the original number:

If $a\%$ is already added to the number, divide the number by $1 + a\%$.

If $a\%$ is subtracted from the number, divide the number by $1 - a\%$.

Examples:

1) If the price was $27 with the sales tax of 8% already added, what was the original price?

$$\frac{27}{1+8\%} = \frac{27}{1.08} = 25$$

Answer: The price was $25.

2) If you pay $80 when you already received a discount of 20%, what was the original purchase price?

$$\frac{80}{1-20\%} = \frac{80}{0.80} = 100$$

Answer: The price was $100.

Practice:

6% tax had been added to my purchase. I paid $106. What was the original purchase price?

Perfect Cubes

Numbers and variables:

Definition: A number or variable that has exactly three equal FACTORS.

Examples:

1) $8 = 2 \times 2 \times 2 = 2^3$

2) $-64 = (-4)(-4)(-4) = (-4)^3$

3) $27a^3 = 3 \times 3 \times 3aaa$

Practice:

Which of the following numbers are perfect cubes: 9, 25, 27, 81, 125?

Algebraic expressions:

Definition: An expression that can be written as a product of three equal factors.

Formulas: $a^3 + 3a^2b + 3ab^2 + b^3 = (a + b)^3$

$a^3 - 3a^2b + 3ab^2 - b^3 = (a - b)^3$

Examples:

1) $x^3 + 3x^2 + 3x + 1 = (x + 1)^3$

2) $a^3 - 6a^2b + 12ab^2 - 8 = (a - 2)^3$

Practice:

Rewrite $x^3 + 9x^2 + 27x + 27$ as a perfect cube.

PERFECT SQUARES

Numbers and variables:

Definition: A number or variable that has exactly two equal factors. Note: A perfect square is always positive.

Examples:

1) $4 = 2 \times 2$

2) $a^4 = a^2a^2$

Practice:

Which of the following are perfect squares: 4, 8, 12, 16, 20?

Algebraic expressions:

Definition: An expression that can be written as the product of two equal factors.

Formulas: $a^2 + 2ab + b^2 = (a + b)^2$
                  $a^2 - 2ab + b^2 = (a - b)^2$

Examples:

1) $x^2 + 2x + 1 = (x + 1)^2$

2) $4x^2 - 12x + 9 = (2x - 3)^2$

Practice:

Write $x^2 + 8x + 16$ as a perfect square.

PERIMETER

Definition: The distance round the edge of a plane figure.

Examples:

1) In w the perimeter
    l $P = l + w + l + w = 2l + 2w.$

2) The perimeter of a circle is called the circumference.

Practice:

Find the perimeter of a square whose side
equals 2 inches.

PERPENDICULAR LINES

Definition: Lines that form right angles when they intersect. The product of the SLOPES of two perpendicular lines equals −1 except when one of the lines has a slope = 0 (see *Example 1b.*)

Examples:

1) *a.* 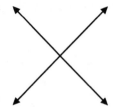 *b.*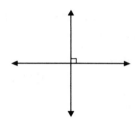

2) The lines $y = 2x + 5$ and $y = -\frac{1}{2}x + 1$ are

   perpendicular, because their slopes are 2 and $-\frac{1}{2}$

   respectively and $2 \times (-\frac{1}{2}) = -1$.

PI (π)

Definition: An IRRATIONAL NUMBER that is the RATIO of the circumference of any circle and its diameter. In other words, the circumference divided by the diameter equals π. Note that both the circumference and the diameter are never whole numbers at the same time. π is approximately (≈) equal to

3.14159... or $\approx \frac{22}{7}$

Example:

   If the circumference of a circle is 12.6 cm and the
   diameter is 4 cm, the ratio between the circumference
   and the diameter is 12.6 ÷ 4 = 3.15, which is
   approximately equal to π.

Pie Graph (Pie Chart)

See CIRCLE GRAPH.

PLACE VALUE

Definition: A position within a number. For example, the place immediately to the left of the decimal point has a value of 1 (the ones or units place).

Whole numbers: ... billions, hundred millions, ten millions, millions, hundred thousands, ten thousands, thousands, hundreds, tens, ones.

Examples:

1) In 6,029,005, the digit 2 is in the ten-thousands place.

2) In 596,005, the digit 6 is in the thousands place.

Practice:

What is the value of the digit 7 in 10,700?

Decimals: Ones, tenths, hundredths, thousandths, ten-thousandths, ...

Examples:

1) In 5.003, the digit 3 is in the thousandths place.

2) In 0.03426, the digit 2 is in the ten-thousandths place.

3) In 145,892.763, the digit 9 is in the tens place and the digit 6 is in the hundredths place.

Practice:

What is the value of the digit 7 in 10.0073?

PLANE

Definition: A flat surface that extends infinitely.

Example:

Plane figures in geometry are two-dimensional (they have length and width).

PLOTTING POINTS

Definition: Marking points on a COORDINATE SYSTEM.

Examples:

1)

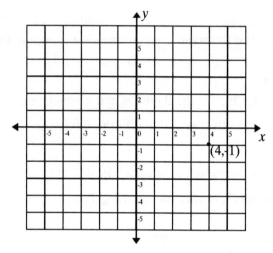

To plot the point $(4,-1)$, start at the ORIGIN (the point where the axes meet), move four steps to the right, continue one step down, and mark the end-point. This is $(4, -1)$.

2) Any point on the *x*-axis has 0 as its second coordinate. Any point on the *y*-axis has 0 as its first coordinate.

Practice:

Plot the points
a) $(3,1)$

b) $(-2,3)$

c) $(0,4)$

POINT

Definition: A location. A point has no size and is defined only by its position.

Symbols: × or ·

In Cartesian COORDINATE SYSTEMS: An ORDERED PAIR represents a point.

Example:

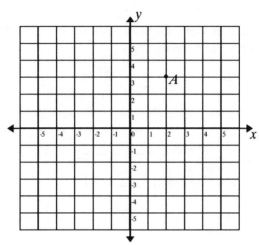

Point $A = (2,3)$

In geometry: A point is represented by the intersection of two lines.

Example:

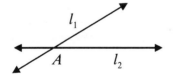

Lines l_1 and l_2 intersect at the point A.

Point-Slope Form

Definition: If a line goes through the point (x_1, y_1) and has a SLOPE (steepness) of m, the equation for the line is:

$y - y_1 = m(x - x_1)$.

Example:

The equation for a line through the point $(1, -2)$ with a slope of 3 is $y - (-2) = 3(x - 1)$ or $y = 3x - 5$.

Practice:

Find the equation of a line with a slope of 1 and which goes through the point $(1,1)$.

POLYGON

Definition: A many-sided plane figure bounded by straight sides.

Examples:

1) A rectangle

2) A hexagon

POLYNOMIALS

Definition: Algebraic expressions with the variables having whole-number (positive) EXPONENTS.

Examples:

1) $3x^2 + 2x - 5$

2) $x^3y^2 - 2x + 3y^2 - 1$

3) $\dfrac{1}{x}$ is not a polynomial. (The exponent of x is -1.)

Polynomials in one variable:

Definition: The terms of the expression contain only one variable. The degree of the polynomial is the highest exponent in any of the terms.

A polynomial of one term is called a monomial.
A polynomial of two terms is called a binomial.
A polynomial of three terms is called a trinomial.

172

Examples:

1) $2x$ is a monomial of degree 1.

2) $x^2 - 5$ is a binomial of degree 2.

3) $3x^2 - 5x + 6$ is a trinomial of degree 2.

4) $x^5 - 4x^4 + 8x^3 + 3x^2 - 9x + 55$ is a polynomial of degree 5.

Practice:

What is the degree of the trinomial $x^5 - 8x^4 + 4x^2$

Operations:

Addition: Add like terms.

Example:

$$(2x^2 + 5x + 3) + (-x^2 + 7x - 5)$$
$$\begin{array}{r} 2x^2 + 5x + 3 \\ \underline{-x^2 + 7x - 5} \\ x^2 + 12x - 2 \end{array}$$

Subtraction: Subtract like terms.

Example:

$$(3x^2 - 2x + 1) - (5x^2 - 8x + 4)$$
$$\begin{array}{r} 3x^2 - 2x + 1 \\ \underline{-5x^2 + 8x - 4} \\ -2x^2 + 6x - 3 \end{array}$$ Remove parentheses and change all signs.

Practice: Subtract:

$$(4x^2 + 3x - 1) - (x^2 - 5x + 1)$$

Multiplication:
1. Monomial times monomial: Multiply coefficients and add exponents.

Example:

$$3a^4b\,(2ab^6) = 6a^{4\,+\,1}b^{1\,+\,6} = 6a^5b^7$$

Practice:

$2a^2b^3(5a^3)$

2. Monomial times binomial: Distribute the monomial over the binomial.

Example:

$3x^3(5x^2 - 4) = 15x^{3+2} - 12x^3 = 15x^5 - 12x^3$

Practice:

$6x^2y^3(2x^3 + xy)$

3. Binomial times binomial: Use FOIL.

Example:

$(x + 1)(2x - 3) = 2x^2 - 3x + 2x - 3 = 2x^2 - x - 3$

Practice:

$(x + 2)(x + 2)$

4. Polynomial times polynomial: Distribute each term from one polynomial over the other polynomial.

Example:

$(a + b + c)(d + e + f) =$
$ad + ae + af + bd + be + bf + cd + ce + cf$

Practice:

$(x + y + 5)(x - y + 2)$

Division:

1. Polynomial divided by monomial: Divide each term by the monomial.

Example:

$(5x^3 - 20x^2 + 25x) \div 5x$

$$\frac{5x^3 - 20x^2 + 25x}{5x} = \frac{5x^3}{5x} - \frac{20x^2}{5x} + \frac{25x}{5x} = x^2 - 4x + 5$$

Practice:

$$\frac{3a+6}{3}$$

2. Polynomial divided by polynomial: Use LONG DIVISION.

Example:

$(x^2 + 5x + 4) \div (x + 1)$

$$
\begin{array}{r}
x + 4 \\
x + 1\overline{)x^2 + 5x + 4} \\
\end{array}
$$

x goes into x^2 x times.

$-x^2 - x$ Multiply $x + 1$ by x and subtract.

$4x + 4$ Carry down 4. x goes into $4x$ 4 times.

$-4x - 4$ Multiply $x + 1$ by 4 and subtract.

Practice:

$$\frac{x^2 + 5x + 6}{x + 2}$$

POSITIVE INTEGERS

Definition: Same as COUNTING NUMBERS.
See also INTEGERS.

Examples:

5 is a positive integer. −5 is a negative integer.

POSITIVE NUMBERS

Definition: All numbers to the right of zero on the number line.

Examples:

$15, 2.6, 1\frac{1}{4}, \pi$

POWER

Definition: The number of times a number is multiplied by itself. See also EXPONENT.

Example:

In $2^4 = 2 \times 2 \times 2 \times 2 = 16$, 16 is the fourth power of two. The exponent in 2^4 is four.

POWERS OF 10

Definition: An EXPONENTIAL NOTATION with 10 as its base.

Examples:

1) $100 = 10^2$

2) $0.001 = 10^{-3}$

Operations:

Multiplication and division: Move the decimal point as many places as the exponent indicates. With multiplication, a positive exponent tells us to move to the right and a negative exponent to the left. With division, a positive exponent tells us to move to the left and a negative exponent to the right.

Examples:

1) $2.6 \times 10^3 = 2600$

2) $568 \times 10^{-2} = 5.68$

3) $150 \div 10^3 = 0.150$

4) $0.06 \div 10^{-2} = 6$

Practice: Evaluate:

a) 0.5×10^{-2}

b) $0.5 \div 10^{-2}$

PREFIX

Definition: One or more letters placed before a word to modify its meaning. Prefixes are used in the METRIC SYSTEM. They are kilo, hecto, deca, deci, centi, and milli and are abbreviated k, h, da, d, c, and m, respectively.

Example:

There are 1000 g in 1 kg.

Prime Factor

Definition: A PRIME NUMBER (a number that can only be divided by 1 and by itself) that divides a number evenly.

Examples:

2 is a prime factor of 6, because $6 \div 2 = 3$.
3 is a prime factor of 6, because $6 \div 3 = 2$.

Practice:

List the prime factors of 20.

Prime Factorization

Definition: To write a whole number as a product of prime factors.

Example:

$72 = 8 \times 9 = 2 \times 4 \times 3 \times 3 = 2 \times 2 \times 2 \times 3 \times 3$

Practice:

Write 20 as a product of prime factors.

Prime Number

Definition: A number that can only be divided by 1 and by itself.

Examples:

2, 3, 5, 7, and 11.
Note that 2 is the only even prime number.

Practice:

Is 31 a prime number?

PRINCIPAL

Definition: Money that is borrowed or saved.
See also INTEREST.

Example:

> If $100 is deposited in the bank with 3% interest,
> $100 is the principal.

PRINCIPAL SQUARE ROOT

Definition: The same as the positive SQUARE ROOT.

Example:

> The equation $x^2 = 4$ has two solutions ($x = 2$ and $x = -2$),
> whereas $\sqrt{4}$ has only one solution: 2, the positive or
> principal square root.

Practice:

> What is the principal square root of 25?

PROBABILITY

Definition: The likelihood that a certain event will occur.
The probability is the ratio of favorable outcomes to total
outcomes.

Example:

> A jar contains 50 jellybeans: 10 pink, 20 white, 5 red, and
> 15 yellow. The probability of picking a pink jellybean is
> $\frac{10}{50}$ or $\frac{1}{5}$, because the favorable outcome (pink) is 10 out
> of a total of 50.

Practice:

> What is the probability of getting a yellow jellybean?

PRODUCT

Definition: The answer in a multiplication problem.

Example:

$2 \times 3 = 6$ (factor × factor = product)

PROPER FRACTION

Definition: A fraction in which the numerator is smaller than the denominator. See FRACTIONS.

Example:

$\frac{2}{3}$ is a proper fraction.

PROPERTIES

See Appendix 3 on page 23.

PROPORTION

Definition: Two equal RATIOS.

Examples:

1) $\frac{2}{5} = \frac{4}{10}$ 2 is to 5 as 4 is to 10.

2) $\frac{1}{3} = \frac{x}{9}$ 1 is to 3 as x is to 9.

   Therefore $x = 3$ because 3 is to 9 as 1 is to 3.

PROTRACTOR

Definition: A device used to measure angles.

Example:

PYTHAGOREAN THEOREM

Definition: The sum of the squares of the legs in a right triangle equals the square of the hypotenuse.

Formula: $a^2 + b^2 = c^2$,

where a and b are legs of a right triangle and c is the hypotenuse.

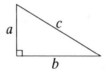

Examples:

1) If $a = 3$ and $b = 4$, then $c = 5$,
   because $3^2 + 4^2 = 9 + 16 = 25 = 5^2$.

2) If $a = 1$ and $b = 1$, then $c = \sqrt{2}$,
   because $1^2 + 1^2 = 1 + 1 = 2 = (\sqrt{2})^2$.

Practice:

Find c when $a = 5$ and $b = 12$.

PYTHAGOREAN TRIPLETS

Definition: Whole numbers a, b, and c that follow the rule: $a^2 + b^2 = c^2$. See PYTHAGOREAN THEOREM.

Examples:

1) 3, 4, 5 because $3^2 + 4^2 = 9 + 16 = 25.$ $(25 = 5^2)$

2) 5, 12, 13 because $5^2 + 12^2 = 25 + 144 = 169.$
   $(169 = 13^2)$

Practice:

Which of the following triplets are Pythagorean:
   2, 3, 4
   6, 8, 10
   8, 15, 17

Quadrants

Definition: The four equal parts created when the COORDI-NATE AXES divide a plane.

Examples:

1)

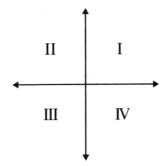

2) The point $(-2,3)$ is in the second quadrant (II).

3) The point $(2,-2)$ is in the fourth quadrant (IV).

Practice:

What is the sign of the *x*-coordinate in quadrant III?

Quadratic Equation

Definition: An equation in one variable raised to the second power. It has two solutions.

Example:

$x^2 + 5x + 6 = 0$ has two solutions: $x = -2$ and $x = -3$.

Solving quadratic equations:

1. By factoring and setting each factor equal to 0.

Example:

$$x^2 + 5x + 6 = 0$$
$$(x + 2)(x + 3) = 0$$

$$x + 2 = 0 \qquad x + 3 = 0$$
$$x = -2 \qquad x = -3$$

181

Check: $(-2)^2 + 5(-2) + 6 = 4 - 10 + 6 = 0$
           $(-3)^2 + 5(-3) + 6 = 9 - 15 + 6 = 0$

2. By formula:

Formula: Equation: $ax^2 + bx + c = 0$

$$x = \frac{-b \pm \sqrt{b^2 - 4ac}}{2a}$$

Example:

$x^2 + 5x + 6 = 0$ $a = 1$ $b = 5$ $c = 6$

$$x = \frac{-5 \pm \sqrt{25 - 4(1)(6)}}{2(1)}$$

$$x = \frac{-5 \pm 1}{2}$$ $x_1 = -2$ $x_2 = -3$

3. By graphing and reading the x-intercepts.

Example:

Solve $x^2 + 5x + 6 = 0$
Graph $y = x^2 + 5x + 6$

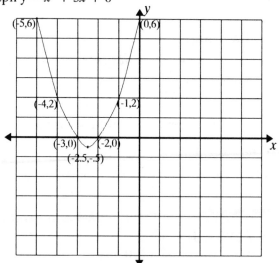

The x-intercepts are -3 and -2.

Practice:

Solve the equation $x^2 + 2x - 3 = 0$ by

a) Factoring.

b) Formula.

c) Graphing.

QUADRATIC FORMULA

Definition: A formula that gives the solution to a second degree equation. See QUADRATIC EQUATIONS.

QUADRILATERAL

Definition: A plane figure with four sides.

Examples:

1) A square

2)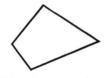

QUOTIENT

Definition: The answer in a division problem.

Example:

In $12 \div 4 = 3$, 3 is the quotient.

Radical

Definition: An expression such as a square root, a cube root, or a general the nth root. See also ROOT.

Symbol: $\sqrt[n]{a}$ where n is a positive integer greater than or equal to 2. a is a real number and positive, if n is even. If n is odd, then a can be negative. n is called the index.

Example:

In $\sqrt{5}$, $\sqrt{}$ is the radical sign and 5 is the RADICAND. The index is understood to be 2.

Operations:

Addition and subtraction: Radicals with the same index and radicands can be added and subtracted.

Examples:

1) $\sqrt{2} + \sqrt{2} = 2\sqrt{2}$

2) $7\sqrt[3]{5} - 3\sqrt[3]{5} = 4\sqrt[3]{5}$

Practice:

Add $2\sqrt[3]{4} + 4\sqrt[3]{4} + \sqrt[3]{4}$

Multiplication and division: Radicals with the same index can be multiplied and divided. See also RATIONALIZATION.

Examples:

1) $\sqrt{2} \cdot \sqrt{2} = \sqrt{4} = 2$

2) $\sqrt[3]{3} \cdot \sqrt[3]{9} = \sqrt[3]{27} = 3$

3) $\dfrac{\sqrt{14}}{\sqrt{7}} = \sqrt{\dfrac{14}{7}} = \sqrt{2}$

4) $\dfrac{\sqrt{75x^5y^3}}{\sqrt{3xy}} = \sqrt{\dfrac{75x^5y^3}{3xy}} = \sqrt{25x^4y^2} = 5x^2y$

Practice: Simplify:

   a) $\sqrt[5]{4} \cdot \sqrt[5]{8}$

   b) $\dfrac{\sqrt[3]{9}}{\sqrt[3]{3}}$

RADICAL EQUATIONS

Definition: Equations that contain a variable in a RADICAND.

Examples:

   1) $\sqrt{x} = 3$

   2) $\sqrt{x-1} = 2$

To solve: Square both sides. Check the solutions in the original equation before it was squared.

Examples:

   1) $\sqrt{x} = 3$
        $(\sqrt{x})^2 = 3^2$
           $x = 9$
      Check: $\sqrt{9} = 3$

   2) $\sqrt{x-1} = 2$
        $(\sqrt{x-1})^2 = 2^2$
          $x-1 = 4$
            $x = 5$
      Check: $\sqrt{5-1} = \sqrt{4} = 2$

   3) $\sqrt{2x-3} = x-3$
       $(\sqrt{2x-3})^2 = (x-3)^2$
         $2x-3 = (x-3)^2$
         $2x-3 = x^2 - 6x + 9$
   See formula for PERFECT SQUARES.

$0 = x^2 - 8x + 12$ Factor:

$0 = (x - 6)(x - 2)$

$x - 6 = 0$ $x - 2 = 0$

    $x = 6$ Solution 1. $x = 2$ Solution 2.

Check 1: $\sqrt{2(6) - 3} = \sqrt{9} = 3$

                            $6 - 3 = 3$

Check 2: $\sqrt{4 - 3} = \sqrt{1} = 1$

                    $2 - 3 = -1$ Reject solution 2.

                                       1 is not the same as -1.

Practice:

Solve $\sqrt{x + 2} = x$

RADICAND

Definition: The number or expression inside the RADICAL.

Examples:

1) In $\sqrt{4}$, 4 is the radicand.

2) In $\sqrt{x - 1}$, $x - 1$ is the radicand.

RADIUS (RADII)

Definition: The distance from the center of a circle to any point on its circumference. The plural of radius is radii.

Example:

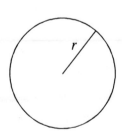

Rate

In percent problems:

Definition: The percentage.

Examples:

1) The rate of the sales tax is 8.25%.

2) The mortgage rates have decreased from 10% to 7%.

In motion problems:

Definition: The speed with which something moves (for cars, it is usually expressed in miles/hour or kilometers /hour).

Examples:

1) The rate of flow was 150 cubic centimeters per hour.

2) The rate of the car was 55 mph (miles per hour).

Rate Problems

Definition: Problems involving movement such as the speed of a car or the flow of water. See also MOTION PROBLEMS and WORK PROBLEMS.

Example:

1) What distance did Jean cover, if she walked for 2 hours at a rate of 4 miles per hour?
    Formula: $d = rt$
    $$d = 4 \times 2 = 8$$
    Answer: 8 miles

2) A pipe can fill a tank in 4 hours. What is the rate?
    Formula: Part of task completed = rate · time
    $$1 = r{\cdot}4$$
    $$r = 1/4$$
    Answer: 1/4 of the tank was filled every hour.

Practice:

> If the rate of the car was 55 miles per hour, how long would it take to drive 220 miles?

RATIO

Definition: A comparison of two numbers by division usually reduced to its simplest terms.

Symbol: **:** or a fraction bar

Examples:

1) 2 : 3 or $\frac{2}{3}$

2) Find the ratio of 2 feet to 3 inches.
   2 ft = 24 in
   The ratio is 24:3 or 8:1

Practice:

> In a class there are 15 girls and 18 boys. What is the ratio of girls to boys?

RATIO AND PROPORTION PROBLEMS

Definition: Problems that deal with RATIOS or PROPORTIONS (two equal ratios).

Ratio problems:

Example:

> Two numbers are in the ratio 3 to 4. Their sum is 35. Find the numbers.
>
> Call the numbers $3x$ and $4x$.
>
> Equation:
> $$3x + 4x = 35$$
> $$7x = 35$$
> $$x = 5$$
> $$3x = 15$$
> $$4x = 20$$

Answer: The numbers are 15 and 20.

Practice:

In a class of 28 pupils, the ratio of boys to girls is 3 : 4. How many girls are there in the class?

Proportion problems:

Template (form):

	Case 1	Case 2
Unit 1		
Unit 2		

Example:

8 quarts of ice cream were used to make 100 milk shakes. How many quarts of ice cream will be needed to make 550 milk shakes?

	Case 1	Case 2
Unit 1	8 qts	x qts
Unit 2	100 shakes	550 shakes

Proportion: $\dfrac{8}{100} = \dfrac{x}{550}$

Cross multiply: $8(550) = 100x$

$x = 44$ Answer: 44 quarts

Practice:

Bill earns $150 in 4 days. How many days will it take him to earn $225?

RATIONAL EQUATIONS

Definition: Equations that contain RATIONAL EXPRESSIONS (that is, ratios (fractions) of numbers and expressions).

Examples:

1) $3 - \dfrac{4}{x} = \dfrac{5}{2}$

2) $\dfrac{3}{x+4} = \dfrac{4}{x-1}$

To solve: Clear the fractions by multiplying each term with the LCD.

If the equations are PROPORTIONS, CROSS MULTIPLY.

Examples:

1) $3 - \dfrac{4}{x} = \dfrac{5}{2}$

   Multiply by the LCD 2x:

   $6x - 8 = 5x$

   $x = 8$

   Check: $3 - \dfrac{4}{8} = 3 - \dfrac{1}{2} = 2\dfrac{1}{2} = \dfrac{5}{2}$

2) $\dfrac{3}{x+4} = \dfrac{4}{x-1}$

   Cross multiply: $3(x - 1) = 4(x + 4)$

   $3x - 3 = 4x + 16$

   $-19 = x$

   Check: $\dfrac{3}{-19+4} = \dfrac{3}{-15} = -\dfrac{1}{5}$

   $\dfrac{4}{-19-1} = \dfrac{4}{-20} = -\dfrac{1}{5}$

Practice:

$\dfrac{1}{2} = \dfrac{1}{x} + \dfrac{1}{6}$

RATIONAL EXPRESSIONS

Definition: Numbers or expressions that can be written as ratios (fractions) of numbers and expressions.

Examples:

1) $\dfrac{2}{x}$

2) $\dfrac{x+5}{x+1}$

Operations:

Reducing to lowest terms: Factor the numerator and denominator completely. Divide both numerator and denominator by any common factors.

Examples:

1) $\dfrac{9}{12} = \dfrac{3 \cdot 3}{3 \cdot 4} = \dfrac{3}{4}$

2) $\dfrac{2x^2}{x^3} = \dfrac{2}{x}$

3) $\dfrac{xy - y^2}{2y} = \dfrac{y(x - y)}{2y} = \dfrac{x - y}{2}$

4) $\dfrac{x^2 + 2x - 3}{x - 1} = \dfrac{(x - 1)(x + 3)}{x - 1} = x + 3$

Practice: Reduce to lowest terms:

$$\dfrac{x^2y + xy^2}{x + y}$$

Addition and subtraction: Find the least common denominator (LCD). Rewrite each fraction as an equivalent fraction with the LCD. Add or subtract the numerators. Reduce, if possible.

Examples:

1) $\dfrac{x}{x + 2} + \dfrac{2}{x + 2} = \dfrac{x + 2}{x + 2} = 1$

2) $\dfrac{3}{2x^2y} + \dfrac{1}{4xy^2}$ LCD $= 4x^2y^2$

   $\dfrac{3}{2x^2y} \cdot \dfrac{2y}{2y} + \dfrac{1}{4xy^2} \cdot \dfrac{x}{x} = \dfrac{6y}{4x^2y^2} + \dfrac{x}{4x^2y^2} = \dfrac{6y + x}{4x^2y^2}$

3) $\dfrac{4}{3x} + \dfrac{2x}{3x + 6} = \dfrac{4}{3x} + \dfrac{2x}{3(x + 2)}$ LCD $= 3x(x + 2)$

In vertical form:

$$\frac{4}{3x} = \frac{4(x+2)}{3x(x+2)}$$

$$+\frac{2x}{3(x+2)} = +\frac{2x^2}{3x(x+2)}$$

$$\frac{4x+8+2x^2}{3x(x+2)} = \frac{2(x^2+2x+4)}{3x(x+2)}$$

Practice:

a) $\dfrac{3x}{2y^2} + \dfrac{1}{4xy}$

b) $\dfrac{3}{2xy^2} - \dfrac{1}{4x^2y}$

Multiplication and division: Factor numerator and denominator. Change the division to multiplication by inverting the divisor (second fraction). Reduce, if possible.

Examples:

1) $\dfrac{2}{3} \times \dfrac{3}{5} = \dfrac{2 \times 3}{3 \times 5} = \dfrac{2}{5}$

2) $\dfrac{4}{5} \div \dfrac{3}{10} = \dfrac{4}{5} \times \dfrac{10}{3} = \dfrac{8}{3}$

3) $\dfrac{2x}{3y} \times \dfrac{3y}{5x} = \dfrac{2}{5}$

4) $\dfrac{3a^2}{7b^2} \div \dfrac{ab}{2} = \dfrac{3a^2}{7b^2} \cdot \dfrac{2}{ab} = \dfrac{6a}{7b^3}$

5) $\dfrac{x^2-4}{x+5} \cdot \dfrac{(x+5)^2}{2x-4} = \dfrac{(x+2)(x-2)(x+5)^2}{(x+5) \cdot 2(x-2)} = \dfrac{(x+2)(x+5)}{2}$

6) $\dfrac{x^2-1}{x+2} \div \dfrac{x-1}{x+2} = \dfrac{(x+1)(x-1)(x+2)}{(x+2)(x-1)} = x+1$

Practice:

a) $\dfrac{3x^2}{2y} \div \dfrac{3x}{4y^3}$

b) $\dfrac{x^2 + 2x}{x} \cdot \dfrac{(x-2)^2}{x^2 - 4}$

RATIONAL NUMBERS

Definition: Any number that can be written as a division of two integers (that is, as a fraction). The divisor cannot be 0.

Examples:

1) $\dfrac{2}{3}, -\dfrac{11}{5}, 2\dfrac{1}{2}, 3.2 = \dfrac{32}{10}$, and $\sqrt{4} = 2$ are rational numbers.

2) $\sqrt{2}, \sqrt{3}$, and π are IRRATIONAL NUMBERS.

Practice:

Show that 7 is a rational number.

RATIONALIZING

Definition: To remove all RADICALS (square roots) from the denominator. This was a useful technique before we had calculators. To get an approximate value of $\dfrac{1}{\sqrt{2}}$ one had to divide 1 by 1.414 (the approximation of $\sqrt{2}$). It is much easier to divide 1.414 by 2.

If the denominator is a monomial (one term) with a square root:

Multiply the numerator and the denominator by a square root that makes the RADICAND (the number below the square root symbol) a perfect square. Because $\sqrt{a^2} = a$ for any positive number, the radical symbol disappears.

Examples:

1) $\dfrac{1}{\sqrt{2}} = \dfrac{1 \cdot \sqrt{2}}{\sqrt{2} \cdot \sqrt{2}} = \dfrac{\sqrt{2}}{\sqrt{4}} = \dfrac{\sqrt{2}}{2}$

2) $\dfrac{3a}{\sqrt{3a}} = \dfrac{3a \cdot \sqrt{3a}}{\sqrt{3a} \cdot \sqrt{3a}} = \dfrac{3a \cdot \sqrt{3a}}{3a} = \sqrt{3a}$

Practice:

Rationalize the denominator: $\dfrac{5}{\sqrt{5}}$

If the denominator is a binomial (two terms) containing at least one square root: Multiply both numerator and denominator by the CONJUGATE (the same numbers as in the binomial but with the opposite operation sign). This is a useful technique in calculus problems, because the radical symbols disappear: $\left(\sqrt{a} + \sqrt{b}\right)\left(\sqrt{a} - \sqrt{b}\right) = (a - b)$.

Thus $\left(\sqrt{3} + \sqrt{2}\right)\left(\sqrt{3} - \sqrt{2}\right) = 3 - 2 = 1$

Examples:

1) $\dfrac{1}{3+\sqrt{2}} = \dfrac{1(3-\sqrt{2})}{(3+\sqrt{2})(3-\sqrt{2})} = \dfrac{3-\sqrt{2}}{9-4} = \dfrac{3-\sqrt{2}}{5}$

2) $\dfrac{\sqrt{3}}{2-\sqrt{3}} = \dfrac{\sqrt{3}(2+\sqrt{3})}{(2-\sqrt{3})(2+\sqrt{3})} =$

$\dfrac{\sqrt{3}(2+\sqrt{3})}{4-3} = \dfrac{2\sqrt{3}+3}{1} = 2\sqrt{3} + 3$

Practice:

Rationalize the denominator: $\dfrac{2}{2+\sqrt{2}}$

Ray

Definition: Part of a line and with one end point.

Examples:

1) Sun ray

2) ├─────────────────→

Reading Numbers

Whole numbers: Separate large numbers into groups of 3 starting from the right. Read each group from left to right. The names of the groups are billions, millions, thousands, and ones. See also PLACE VALUE.

Examples:

1) 45,035 is read as forty-five thousand, thirty-five.

2) 385,023,865,015 is read as three hundred eighty-five billion, twenty-three million, eight hundred sixty-five thousand, fifteen.

Practice:

Write 105,206 in words.

Decimal numbers: The decimal point is read as "and" or as "point." The decimals are read as whole numbers followed by the name of the rightmost place.

Examples:

1) 5.025 is read as five and twenty-five thousandths or as five point zero two five.

2) 0.00003 is read as three hundred-thousandths or as zero point zero zero zero zero three.

Practice:

Write 12.025 in words.

Real Numbers

Definition: All numbers that can be found on the number line. Non-real numbers are IMAGINARY.

Examples:

1) $2, 0.6, -0.0047, -\frac{35}{93}, \sqrt{2}$, and π are real numbers.

2) $\sqrt{-4}$ is an imaginary number.

Practice:

Why is $-\sqrt{4}$ a real number?

Reciprocal

Definition: The product of a number and its reciprocal equals one. Reciprocals are also called INVERSES.

Example:

$$\frac{2}{3} \times \frac{3}{2} = \frac{6}{6} = 1 \qquad \frac{2}{3} \text{ and } \frac{3}{2} \text{ are reciprocals.}$$

Rectangle

Definition: A four-sided figure with opposite sides equal and with all angles 90°.

Examples:

1)

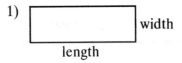

length

2) A rectangle with equal sides is a square.

Practice:

Is a square a rectangle?

RECTANGULAR COORDINATE SYSTEM

See the CARTESIAN COORDINATE SYSTEM.

REDUCING FRACTIONS

Definition: Dividing the numerator and denominator by common factors.
See also FRACTIONS and RATIONAL EXPRESSIONS.

Examples:

1) $\frac{4}{16} = \frac{1}{4}$ This is obtained by dividing numerator and denominator by 4.

2) $\frac{(x+2)^2}{x^2-4} = \frac{(x+2)(x+2)}{(x+2)(x-2)} = \frac{x+2}{x-2}$

Practice:

Reduce the following fractions:

a) $\frac{10}{15}$

b) $\frac{3x^2y^5}{6xy^6}$

REFLECTION

Definition: A mirror image of a figure. See also AXIS.

Example:

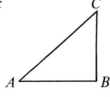 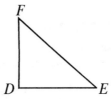

The image of triangle *ABC* is triangle *DEF*.

Regular Polygons

Definition: A polygon (many-sided figure) with all sides equal and all angles equal.

Examples:

1) A square.   Each angle is 90°.

2) An equilateral triangle.   Each angle is 60°.

Related Pairs

Definition: Two numbers that are connected by a rule.

Example:

The ORDERED PAIRS (1,3), (2,4), and (3,5) are connected by the rule $y = x + 2$.

Remainder

Definition: The whole number that is left over after a division of whole numbers.

Example:

$17 \div 4 = 4$ R1   1 is the remainder.

Repeating Decimals

Definition: Decimals that never end but have groups of decimals that are repeated forever.

Symbol: ... or a bar over the repeating group.

Examples:

1) 0.1212... or $0.\overline{12}$

2) 0.185185... or $0.\overline{185}$

3) $\sqrt{2} \approx 1.4142135...$ is a non-repeating decimal.

Practice:

What is the repeating group in 0.63636...?

RHOMBUS

Definition: A quadrilateral (four-sided figure) with equal sides. The angles are usually not equal to 90°, but they could be according to the definition.

Example:

Practice:

What is the name of a rhombus with 90° angles?

RIGHT ANGLE

Definition: A 90° angle. It is marked with a small square.

Example:

RIGHT TRIANGLE

Definition: A triangle with one right angle. The sides forming the right angle are called legs (often designated with the letters a and b). The side opposite the right angle is the hypotenuse (designated with the letter c).

Example:

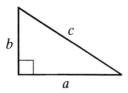

ROOT

In equations:

Definition: Solution to an equation. The root satisfies the equation—that is, makes a true statement when the variable is replaced with the root.

Examples:

1) 2 is a root to the equation $x + 3 = 5$, because $2 + 3 = 5$.

2) 1 and 2 are roots to the equation $x^2 - 3x + 2 = 0$, because $1 - 3 + 2 = 0$ and $4 - 6 + 2 = 0$.

Practice:

Is 3 a root to the equation $x - 3 = 1$?

In exponential notation:

Definition: The INVERSE of an exponential expression. If, for example, the square root of 2 is squared, the operations cancel each other out, and the answer is 2.

Symbol: $\sqrt[n]{}$

$\sqrt[n]{a^n} = a$ where n is a positive integer (whole number $\neq 0$) and is called the INDEX. a is a positive number if n is even.

Examples:

1) $\sqrt{9}$ is pronounced "square root of 9" or "radical 9."

2) $\sqrt[5]{2^5} = 2$ and $\sqrt[3]{6^3} = 6$

Practice:

Find the $\sqrt[3]{64}$.

ROUNDING

Definition: Approximating a number by adjusting the last digit in a number up or down after some digits have been dropped. Often it is enough to know, for example, that a number is roughly 5,000 instead of knowing that is exactly 4,875.

For whole numbers: If the digit to the right of the rounded digit is less than five, leave the digit the same. If the digit to the right of the rounded digit is five or more, increase the rounded digit by one. Replace the dropped digits by zeros.

Example:

Round 4,685 to the nearest hundred. 46|85. Add 1 to 6 and replace 8 and 5 with zeros. $4{,}685 \approx 4{,}700$

Practice:

Round 59,830 to the nearest thousand.

For decimals: If the digit to the right of the rounded digit is less than five, leave the digit the same. If the digit to the right of the rounded digit is five or more, increase the first digit by one. Discard all digits to the right of the rounded digit.

Examples:

1) Round 3.0467 to the nearest hundredth.
   $3.04|67 \approx 3.05$

2) Round 15.984 to the nearest tenth.
   $15.9|84 \approx 16.0$ This zero should not be dropped. It is in the tenths place.

Practice:

Round 24.36842 to the nearest thousandth.

Satisfy An Equation

Definition: To find numbers that, when they replace the variables in the equation, give a true statement.

Example:

$x = 2$ satisfies the equation $2x - 1 = 3$
because $2(2) - 1 = 3$.

Practice:

Show that $x = 1$ satisfies the equation $2x + 1 = 3$.

Scales

Definition: The distance between the numbers on a number line.

Examples:

1)

-5 -4 -3 -2 -1 0 1 2 3 4 5
One unit = 0.5 cm.

2)

-10 -8 -6 -4 -2 0 2 4 6 8 10
One unit = 0.25 cm.

Practice:

Make a number line with one unit = 1 inch.

Scientific Notation

Definition: A number written as a product of a number greater than one and less than 10 and a power of 10. See also POWERS OF 10. This notation is used by scientists and engineers working with very large or very small numbers.

Examples:

1) $456 = 4.56 \times 10^2$ The decimal point was moved two steps.

2) $0.00035 = 3.5 \times 10^{-4}$ The decimal point was moved four steps.

Practice:

Write 54,690 in scientific notation.

Secant

Definition: A line that intersects a curve in two points. See also CHORD.

Example:

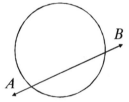

The line *AB* is a secant to the circle.

Sector

Definition: A part of a circle that is bordered by two radii and the arc, which is formed by these radii.

Example:

SEGMENT

Of a line:

Definition: A piece of a straight line with a beginning and an end.

Example:

A   B $\overline{AB}$ is a line segment.

Of a circle:

Definition: A part of a circle that is bordered by a chord and the arc, which is formed by the chord.

Example:

SEMICIRCLE

Definition: A half-circle.

Example:

SET

Definition: A collection of things.

Symbol: { } (braces).

Example:

The set of whole numbers: {0, 1, 2, ...}

SIGNED NUMBERS

Definition: Numbers preceded by a positive or negative sign. See also INTEGERS.

Examples:

$$+2, -5, +0.6, -\frac{2}{3}$$

SIMILAR FIGURES

Definition: Geometric figures with the same shape but with different size.

Symbol: ~

Example:

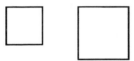

SIMILARITY RATIO

Definition: The ratio between corresponding sides in similar figures.

Example:

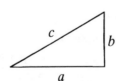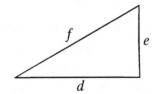

If the triangles are similar, then the similarity ratio is

$$\frac{a}{d} = \frac{b}{e} = \frac{c}{f} \cdot$$

SIMPLE INTEREST

See INTEREST.

SIMPLIFY

Definition: To perform all operations in order to make an expression simpler and shorter. It essentially means "do what you are told" and follow the rules for ORDER OF OPERATIONS and COMBINING LIKE TERMS.

Examples:

1) $2(3) + 6 \div 2 = 6 + 3 = 9$

2) $5x - x(2 - x) = 5x - 2x + x^2 = x^2 + 3x$

3) $\dfrac{25x^5}{5x^2} + \dfrac{12x^4}{6x} = 5x^3 + 2x^3 = 7x^3$

Practice:

Simplify: $2ab^3(5a^2b^4)$

SIMULTANEOUS EQUATIONS

Definition: Two or more equations that are true at the same time.

Example:

$5x + 2y = 9$ and $3x - 2y = -1$ have a common solution: $x = 1$ and $y = 2$.

Methods for solving simultaneous equations:

<u>Method 1</u>. Addition (Elimination) method

Multiply one or both equations with numbers that make the coefficients of one variable opposite numbers. (They have the same size but one is plus and one is minus.) Add the equations. One variable will be eliminated. Solve for the remaining variable. Replace the solution in one of the original equations and solve.

Examples:

1) Solve:
$$x + y = 5$$
$$x - y = 3$$

Add the equations:
$$2x = 8$$
$$x = 4$$

Replace x in first equation:
$$4 + y = 5$$
$$y = 1$$

Check the answer in the second equation: $4 - 1 = 3$

2) Solve:
$$2x + 3y = 7$$
$$3x + 2y = 8$$

Multiply the first equation by -2: $\quad -4x - 6y = -14$
Multiply the second equation by 3: $\quad 9x + 6y = 24$
Add the equations:
$$5x = 10$$
$$x = 2$$

Replace x in first equation: $\quad 2(2) + 3y = 7$
Solve: $\quad y = 1$

Check the answer in the second equation:
$$3(2) + 2(1) = 8$$
or in the first equation: $\quad 2(2) + 3(1) = 7$

Practice:

Solve *Example 2* by eliminating x first.

Method 2. Substitution method

Solve for one of the variables in one equation. Use that expression instead of this variable in the other equation. Solve for the second variable. Replace the value for the second variable and solve for the first variable.

Example:

Solve:
$$x + y = 5$$
$$x - y = 3$$

Solve for y: $\quad y = -x + 5$
Replace: $\quad x - (-x + 5) = 3$
$$2x - 5 = 3$$
$$x = 4$$
$$y = -4 + 5 = 1$$

207

To check your solutions replace both variables in each equation by your solutions and see if they come out correctly.

Check: $4 + 1 = 5$
$4 - 1 = 3$

Practice:

Solve the equations in the preceding example by first solving for *x* in one of the equations.

<u>Method 3</u>. Graphing

Graph each equation and determine the point of intersection. This method is not as accurate as the other two, because it is impossible to construct the graph exactly. However, it is useful with other types of equations (such as QUADRATIC EQUATIONS).

Example:

Solve: $x + y = 5$
$x - y = 3$
$x = 4$
$y = 1$

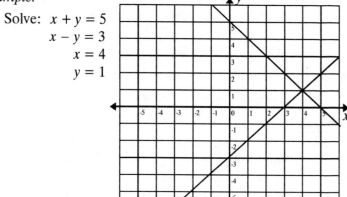

Practice:

Solve $x + 2y = 5$
$x - y = 2$
by using all three methods.

208

SLOPE

Definition: Slope is a measure of the steepness of a line. Two points on the line are selected and the change (difference) in y is divided by the change (difference) in x.

$$m = \frac{y_2 - y_1}{x_2 - x_1}$$

The slope m of a line can also be found from the equation $y = mx + b$, where m is the slope.

Examples:

1) The slope of the line between the points (1,5) and (7,8) is:
   $$m = \frac{8-5}{7-1} = \frac{3}{6} = \frac{1}{2}$$

2) The slope of the line $y = -2x + 5$ is –2.

Practice:

a) Find the slope of the line that connects the points (3,2) and (1,0)

b) What is the slope of the line $y = x + 3$?

SLOPE-INTERCEPT FORM

Definition: The equation of a line when the SLOPE (steepness) m and the Y-INTERCEPT (where the line intersects the y-axis) b are known.

Formula: $y = mx + b$

Example:

Find the equation for a line with a slope of –1 and a y-intercept of –3.
$$m = -1$$
$$b = -3$$
$$y = -x - 3$$

Practice:

Find the equation for a line with a *y*-intercept of 2 and a slope of 3.

SOLVING LINEAR EQUATIONS

Definition: Figuring out what number the variable stands for in an equation. Any operation may be performed on an equation as long as the same operation is performed on both sides of the equation.

Whole numbers:

The simplest equations require only one step to follow.

Examples:

1) $3x = 15$ Divide both sides by 3. $x = 5$

2) $x + 5 = 20$ Subtract 5 from both sides. $x = 15$

More complex equations require more than one step.

Example:

$3x + 5 = 20$ Subtract 5 from both sides.
$3x = 15$ Divide by 3.
$x = 5$

Note: In solving equations we do addition/subtraction before multiplication/division.

If either side of the equation can be simplified, do so.

Example:

In $3x + 2x = 30$, combine like terms:
$5x = 30$ Divide by 5
$x = 6$

If the variable occurs on both sides of the equation, add or subtract one variable term to make it disappear from one side.

Example:

In $10x + 1 = 9x + 10$, subtract $9x$ from both sides:

$x + 1 = 10$ Subtract 1 from both sides.

$x = 9$

Practice: Solve*:*

    a) $5x + 3 = 2x + 9$

    b) $4 + 8x = 36$

    c) $\frac{x}{5} = 2$

Fractions:

If the equation contains fractions, multiply each term by the LEAST COMMON DENOMINATOR (LCD).

Example:

$\frac{x}{2} + \frac{x}{3} = 5$ LCD = 6

Multiply by 6: $3x + 2x = 30$

Solve: $5x = 30$

                 $x = 6$

Practice:

Eliminate the denominators and solve: $\frac{x}{3} - \frac{x}{5} = 2$

Decimals:

If the equation contains decimals, multiply each term with a POWER OF 10 so all decimals become whole numbers

Example:

$$0.1x + 0.01 = 0.09x + 0.1$$

Multiply by 100: $10x + 1 = 9x + 10$

Solve: $x + 1 = 10$

               $x = 9$

Practice:

Eliminate the decimals and solve:
$1x - 0.5x = 0.14 + 0.3x$

General:

Check the solution by substituting the solution in the original equation.

Examples:

1) $\frac{x}{2} + \frac{x}{3} = 5$ $x = 6$

   $\frac{6}{2} + \frac{6}{3} = 3 + 2 = 5$

2) $0.1x + 0.01 = 0.09x + 0.1$ $x = 9$
   Left side: $0.1(9) + 0.01 = 0.9 + 0.01 = 0.91$
   Right side: $0.09(9) + 0.1 = 0.81 + 0.1 = 0.91$

Practice:

Solve and check the solutions:

a) $5x + 3 = 2x + 9$

b) $7x - 3 = 25$

c) $\frac{x}{3} = 1$

d) $\frac{x}{5} + \frac{x}{15} = 4$

e) $x - 0.15x = 2.1 + 0.15x$

SQUARE

In exponential notation:

Definition: The second power of a number, a variable, or an expression.

Formulas for BINOMIAL squares:

$$(a + b)^2 = a^2 + 2ab + b^2$$
$$(a - b)^2 = a^2 - 2ab + b^2$$

These formulas can be derived from multiplying:

$$(a + b)^2 = (a + b)(a + b) = aa + ab + ba + bb$$
$$= a^2 + 2ab + b^2$$

Note $2ab$, which is called the double product.

Examples:

1) $3^2 = 3 \times 3$

2) $x^2 = xx$

3) $(x + 1)^2 = x^2 + 2x + 1$

4) $(2x - 3)^2 = 4x^2 - 12x + 9$

Practice:

Rewrite $(3x - 2)^2$ as a trinomial.

In geometry:

Definition: A plane figure with four equal sides and right angles.

Example:

SQUARE ROOT

Definition: A number that when multiplied by itself yields the original number. The square root has an INDEX of 2. See also RADICALS.

Symbol: $\sqrt{}$

Examples:

1) The square root of 9 is 3, because $3 \times 3 = 9$.

2) $\sqrt{36} = 6$, because $6 \times 6 = 36$.

213

Practice:

What is the square root of 169?

STATISTICS

Definition: Methods of collecting, analyzing and predicting events. See MEAN, MEDIAN, and MODE.

Examples:

1) **Descriptive** statistics deals with collecting and analyzing data.

2) **Inferential** statistics deals with predicting events from known data.

SUBSTITUTE

Definition: To replace a variable with a number. Put parentheses around the variable before you substitute.

Example:

In $2a - 3b$ substitute -1 for a and -2 for b.
$2(-1) - 3(-2) = -2 + 6 = 4$

Practice:

Substitute 3 for x and 4 for y in $3x + 2y^2$.

SUBSTITUTION METHOD

Definition: A method for solving equations that are true at the same time. See SIMULTANEOUS EQUATIONS.

SUBTRACTION

Definition: The reverse of addition.

Example:

$7 - 4 = 3$

SUM

Definition: The answer in addition.

Examples:

1) $4 + 5 = 9$ 9 is the sum.

2) The sum of $2a$ and $6a$ is $8a$.

SUPPLEMENTARY ANGLES

Definition: Two angles whose measures add up to 180°.

Example:

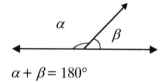

$\alpha + \beta = 180°$

SYMBOL

Definition: Something that represents a concept.

Examples:

1) $ is the symbol for dollar.

2) Numerals are symbols for numbers.

SYMMETRIC

Definition: A figure that can be divided into two parts, each of which is a mirror image of the other.

Examples:

1) The letter A is symmetric.

2) The letter R is not symmetric.

SYSTEM OF EQUATIONS

Same as SIMULTANEOUS EQUATIONS.

TALLY

Definition: Marks used for counting.

Example:

    |||| | equals 6.

TANGENT

Definition: A line that touches a curve at one point. Tangent also means the ratio of the legs of a right triangle.

Examples:

   1)

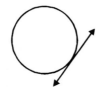

   2)

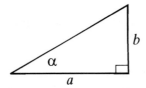

    The tangent of the angle α equals $\dfrac{b}{a}$.

TEMPERATURE

Definition: The degree of hotness or coldness measured on a definite scale. The most common temperature scales are CELSIUS and FAHRENHEIT.

Conversions:

    Water boils at 100° Celsius (C), which corresponds to 212° Fahrenheit (F).
    Water freezes at 0°C, which corresponds to 32°F.

T

Celsius-to-Fahrenheit conversion shortcut:
Multiply by 2, add 30.
Fahrenheit-to-Celsius conversion shortcut:
Subtract 30, divide by 2.

From Celsius to Fahrenheit:

Formula: $F = \dfrac{9}{5}C + 32$

Example:

Convert 10°*C* to Fahrenheit.

$$F = \frac{9}{5}(10) + 32 = 18 + 32 = 50°F$$

From Fahrenheit to Celsius:

Formula: $C = \dfrac{5}{9}(F - 32)$

Example:

Convert 14°*F* to Celsius.

$$C = \frac{5}{9}(14 - 32) = \frac{5}{9}(-18) = -10°C$$

Practice:

Convert by using first the shortcut and then the formula.
a) 25°*C* to *F*°
b) 80°*F* to *C*°

TERM

Definition: The building blocks of addition. See LIKE TERMS and COMBINING LIKE TERMS.

Examples:

1) In 5 + 8 = 13, 5 and 8 are terms.

2) In $3a^2b + 5ab^2$, $3a^2b$ and $5ab^2$ are terms.

TERMINATING DECIMALS

Definition: A decimal number that ends after a certain digit. See DECIMAL NUMBERS.

Example:

　0.45　(0.11111... is a non-terminating decimal.)

TRANSLATIONS

See Appendix 2 on page 21.

TRANSVERSAL

Definition: A line that intersects two other lines.

Example:

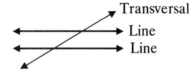

TRAPEZOID

Definition: A four-sided figure with one set of parallel sides.

Example:

TRIANGLE

Definition A three-sided figure.

Example:

TRINOMIAL

Definition: A POLYNOMIAL (an addition/subtraction involving variables) with three TERMS.

Example:

　$x^2 + 5x + 6$

U
V

UNDEFINED

In Arithmetic and Algebra:

Definition: Something that does not exist.

Example:

$6 \div 0$ has no answer. If there was an answer, say a, then $6 = 0 \times a$, which equals 0. That would mean that 6 is equal to 0, and it is not.

In Geometry:

Definition: Terms that are used without definition. They are described and used to define other terms.

Example:

Point, line, and plane are undefined.

UNIT

Definition: A reference value used to express the quantity one. There are units of length, weight, volume, pressure, temperature, and everything else that can be measured.

Examples:

1) A unit of measuring length in the METRIC SYSTEM is the meter.

2) If |—| represents 1, then |—|—| represents 2.

Practice:

If three oranges cost 99 cents, what is the unit price?

VARIABLE

Definition: A letter that can stand for any number. See also EXPONENTS.

Example:

In $3x$, x can have any value, but in $3x = 6$, x stands for 2.

Operations:

Addition and subtraction: Variables that are LIKE TERMS (letters and exponents match) can be added and subtracted.

Examples:

1) $2a + 3a = 5a$

2) $5xy^2 - 5x^2y$ cannot be combined.

Multiplication: Multiply the COEFFICIENTS (the number in front of the variables) and add the EXPONENTS (powers) when the BASES (the number that is raised to a power) are equal.

Example:

$2a^2 \cdot 3a = 6a^3$

Division: Divide the coefficients and subtract the exponents when the bases are equal.

Example:

$10x^2 \div (5x) = 2x$

VERTEX (VERTICES)

Definition: A point that is common to two lines in an angle or a polygon. The plural form of vertex is vertices. An angle has one vertex, a triangle has three vertices and a square has four vertices.

Example:

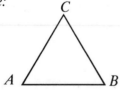

Points A, B, and C are vertices.

VERTICAL ANGLES

Definition: Angles that are opposite of each other when two lines intersect.

Example:

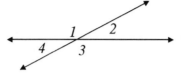

Angles *1* and *3* are vertical angles.
Angles *2* and *4* are vertical angles.

VERTICAL LINES

Definition: Lines that are PERPENDICULAR (at right angle) to the horizon or the ground. The equation of a vertical line is $x = a$, where a is a real number (usually an integer).

Example:

Graph $x = 5$

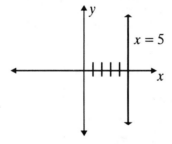

VOLUME

Definition: The extent of space occupied by a solid, a liquid or a gas. Volume of a solid is measured in cubic length units. Volume of a liquid or a gas is measured in cubic liquid units. See the METRIC SYSTEM.

Example:

1) The volume of a box is measured as
   length × width × height.
2) The volume of a bottle of water is measured in liters.
3) The volume of a propane tank is measured in gallons.

WEIGHT

Definition: The force by which an object is attracted by the Earth. Mass and weight are used interchangeably in everyday language.

Example:

> The weight of a person is measured on a scale in units of pounds or kilograms.

WHOLE NUMBERS

Definition: The set of numbers {0, 1, 2, 3,...}. It consists of all the counting numbers and zero. See also PLACE VALUES, READING NUMBERS, and COUNTING NUMBERS.

Example:

> 1) 0 is a whole number but not a counting number.
>
> 2) 1 is both a whole number and a counting number.

Practice:

> Give an example of a number that is not a whole number.

WORD PROBLEMS

Step 1. Read the problem *carefully*. Draw a picture, if possible. Use a template if it is appropriate.

Step 2. Read the problem again and list the quantities you are given and those you are looking for.

Step 3. If possible, make an estimate of what you expect the answer to be.

Step 4. Express each of the unknown quantities in terms of the variable.

Step 5. Write an equation.

Step 6. Solve the equation.

Step 7. Make sure you have found values for all listed unknown quantities.

Step 8. Check the answer. Even if your answer solves the equation you wrote, ask yourself if it makes sense.

Step 9. Re-read the question. Have you answered the question completely or do you have to continue with more calculations?

WORK PROBLEMS

Definition: Problems that involve people or machines working together.

Template:

	Rate of work	Time worked	Part of task
Case 1	Multiply →		↓ Add
Case 2			
			Total = 1

Examples:

1) Mr. Lee can paint a house by himself in 20 hours. Mr. Danko can paint the same house by himself in 30 hours. How long will it take them to paint the house if they work together?

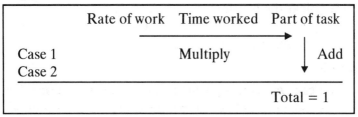

	Rate of work	Time	Part of task
Mr. Lee	1/20 per hr	x hrs	$\dfrac{x}{20}$
Mr. Danko	1/30 per hr	x hrs	$\dfrac{x}{30}$

Equation: $\dfrac{x}{20} + \dfrac{x}{30} = 1$ (One is the whole task.)

Clear fractions: $3x + 2x = 60$

$$x = 12$$

Answer: 12 hours

2) A tank can be filled by one pipe in four hours and emptied by another pipe in six hours. If the valves to both pipes are open, how long will it take to fill the tank?

	Rate	Time	Part of task
Pipe 1	1/4 per hr	x hrs	$\dfrac{x}{4}$
Pipe 2	–1/6 per hr	x hrs	$-\dfrac{x}{6}$

Equation: $\dfrac{x}{4} - \dfrac{x}{6} = 1$

Clear the fractions: $3x - 2x = 12$
$$x = 12$$

Answer: 12 hours

Practice:

Lisa can complete a job in 45 minutes working alone. Brit takes 30 minutes to complete the same job. How long will it take if they work together?

X-Axis

Definition: The HORIZONTAL AXIS (parallel to the ground) in a COORDINATE SYSTEM.

Example:

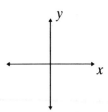

The equation of the x-axis is $y = 0$.

X-Coordinate

Definition: The first number in an ORDERED PAIR (two numbers that are related by a rule).

Example:

The *x*-coordinate in (2,7) is 2.

X-INTERCEPT

Definition: The value of *x* at the point where the line crosses the *x*-axis. See also INTERCEPTS. The *x*-intercept can be found by setting $y = 0$.

Examples:

1) In $x + y = 5$, the *x*-intercept is 5.

2) In $y = mx + b$, the *x*-intercept is $-b/m$.

3)

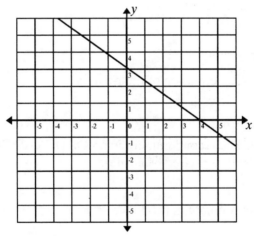

The *x*-intercept is 4.

Practice:

Find the *x*-intercept in $y = 3x - 9$.

X-VALUE

Definition: The value of the variable *x* or the first number in an ordered pair.

Examples:

1) The *x*-value in (2,7) is 2.

2) Find the *x*-value if $y = 2$ and the equation is $x + y = 6$.
   Solution: $x = 4$

Y-Axis

Definition: The VERTICAL (making a right angle with the ground) axis in a coordinate system.

Example:

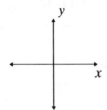

The equation of the *y*-axis is $x = 0$.

Y-Coordinate

Definition: The second number in an ORDERED PAIR (two numbers that are related by a rule).

Example:

The *y*-coordinate in (2,7) is 7.

Y-Intercept

Definition: The value of *y* at the point where the line crosses the *y*-axis. The *y*-intercept can be found by setting $x = 0$. See also INTERCEPTS.

Examples:

1) In $x + y = 5$ the *y*-intercept is 5.

2) In $y = mx + b$ the *y*-intercept is *b*.

3)

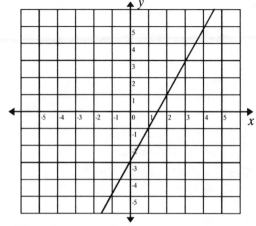

The *y*-intercept is -3.

Practice:

What is the *y*-intercept in $y = 3x - 6$?

Y-VALUE

Definition: The value of the variable *y* or the second number in an ordered pair.

Examples:

1) The *y*-value in (2,7) is 7.

2) Find the *y*-value if $x = 4$ and the equation is $x + y = 6$.
   Answer: $y = 2$.

ZERO

Definition: Zero often means "nothing," but it is also a place-holder in numbers. It is the smallest whole number. It is the IDENTITY element because if you add 0 to a number, the number stays the same.

On the number line, 0 lies between 1 and −1, 2 and −2 etc.; in other words, it is between a number and its opposite. When a number and its opposite are added, the sum is 0.

Operations:

Addition: $a + 0 = a$

Example:

  $3 + 0 = 3$

Subtraction: $a - 0 = a$

Example:

  $8 - 0 = 8$

Multiplication: $a \times 0 = 0$ and $0 \times a = 0$

Example:

  $9 \times 0 = 0$ and $0 \times 9 = 0$

Division: 0 divided by any number (except zero) is 0. Division by 0 is UNDEFINED.

Examples:

  1) $0 \div 6 = 0$

  2) $25 \div 0$ is undefined. It cannot be done.

  3) $0 \div 0$ is INDETERMINATE. It can be any number.

Practice:

  What answer does the calculator give to the examples above?

Power: Any non-zero number to the 0th power is equal to 1. 0^0 is indeterminate.

Examples:

  1) $5^0 = 1$

  2) $2^0 + 3^0 = 1 + 1 = 2$

Practice:

  What is $2^0 \times 3^0$?

Abscissa
   a) 4   *b*) 3

Absolute value
   a) 8   *b*) 7   *c*) 4

Addition method
   a) $x = 4,\ y = 2$ *b*) $x = 1,\ y = 3$ *c*) $x = 3,\ y = 5$

Age problems

  a)

Name	Age now	Age in 3 years
Fritz	x	$x + 3$
Marianne	$x + 5$	$x + 8$

      Equation: $x + 8 = 2(x + 3)$
                    $x + 8 = 2x + 6$
                    $2 = x$
                    $x + 5 = 7$

    Fritz is 2 years old. Maryanne is 7 years old

  b)

Name	Age now	Age 10 years ago
Eva	x	$x - 10$
Brita	$x + 30$	$x + 20$

      Equation: $x + 20 = 2(x - 10)$
                    $x + 20 = 2x - 20$
                    $40 = x$

    Eva is 40 years old

Alternate angles

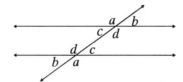

Altitude

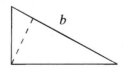

APPROXIMATION

$$1863 + 4828 \approx 2000 + 5000 = 7000$$
$$1863 + 4828 \approx 1900 + 4800 = 6700$$
Correct answer: 6691

AREA

Square is 1 square inch.

Semicircle is $\frac{1}{2}\pi\left(\frac{1}{2}\right)^2 = \frac{\pi}{8} \approx \frac{3.14}{8} \approx 0.4$

Total: 1.4 square inches

ASSOCIATIVE LAW

a) $(25 + 13) + 12 = 38 + 12 = 50;$
$25 + (13 + 12) = 25 + 25 = 50$

b) $(3)(2)(5) = 6(5) = 30;$ $(3)(2)(5) = 3(10) = 30$

AVERAGE

a) $\frac{1+2+2+4+6}{5} = \frac{15}{5} = 3$

b) 90 liters $\div$ 5 = 18 liters

AXIS (AXES)

BAR GRAPH

10

BASE

Percent

a) 30

b) 20

c) 80% of the original price is $40.
$40 \div 0.80 = $50
The original price was $50.

Geometry

Exponential notation

a) 5 *b*) –7 *c*) *x*

Numeration system

0, 1, 2, 3, 4, 5, 6, 7

BINARY

a) 11 001 *b*) 110

CARTESIAN COORDINATE SYSTEM

III; C:(–5, –1); D:(3, 0)

CENTI-

100

CENTRAL ANGLE

∠ *SOT*

CHORD

Yes, it is called a diameter.

CIRCLE

Circumference = $2\pi r = 8\pi$ inches ≈ 25.13 inches
Area = $\pi r^2 = 16\,\pi$ square inches ≈ 50.27 square inches

CIRCLE GRAPH

50% ≈ 180°
25% ≈ 90°
15% ≈ 54°
10% ≈ 36°

CIRCUMFERENCE

$2\pi r = 2\pi(4)$ cm = 8π cm ≈ 25.13 cm

COEFFICIENT

–4

231

COLLINEAR

No, because the slopes are different. $\frac{7-3}{2-0} = \frac{4}{2} = 2$ $\frac{3+2}{0+1} = 5$

COMBINING LIKE TERMS

$5xy^2 + 8xy$

COMMON DENOMINATOR

10, 20, 30

COMMON FACTOR

3, 5, and 15

COMMON MULTIPLE

Multiples of 6: 6, 12, 18, 24, 30, 36, 42, 48, 54, ...
Multiples of 9: 9, 18, 27, 36, 45, 54, ...
Common multiples are: 18, 36, 54, ...

COMPLETING THE SQUARE

a)   16   b)   14

COMPLEX FRACTIONS

$5 \div \frac{11}{15} = 5 \times \frac{15}{11} = \frac{75}{11}$

COMPOUND INTEREST

a) $P = \$200$ $r = 4\%/12$ $t = 12 \times 20 = 240$
  $A = \$200(1 + 0.00333)^{240} = \$444.16$ $I = \$244.16$

b) $P = \$200$ $r = 4\%$ $t = 20$
  $A = \$200(1 + 0.04)^{20} = \$438.22$ $I = \$238.27$

CONJUGATE LAW

a) $(80 + 1)(80 - 1) = 80^2 - 1^2 = 6400 - 1 = 6399$
b)   The conjugate is $2a + 1$: $(2a - 1)(2a + 1) = 4a^2 - 1$

COORDINATE GEOMETRY

b   (Both variables have the exponent 1.)

CROSS-MULTIPLICATION

$2(9) = 18; \ 3(6) = 18$

CUBE

Geometry

a) 6 faces with an area of 1 square inch each.
Total is 6 square inches.

b) $l \times w \times h = 1 \times 1 \times 1 = 1$ cubic inch

Exponential notation

$6 \times 6 \times 6 = 216$

CUBE ROOT

4 because $4 \times 4 \times 4 = 64$

CUSTOMARY (ENGLISH) SYSTEM OF MEASUREMENT

a) 1 yard = 3 feet = 3×12 inches = 36 inches
b) 3×16 oz = 48 oz
c) 32 fluid ounces = 2 pints; 16 fluid ounces = 1 pint.

DECA-

1 dag

DECI-

100 dg

DECIMAL NUMBERS

Reading

a) forty-five and one hundredth;
b) one hundred five thousandths

Decimals to fractions

$32.125 = 32\frac{125}{1000} = 32\frac{1}{8}$

Fractions to decimals

$\frac{1}{4} = 1 \div 4 = 0.25 \qquad 1\frac{1}{4} = 1.25$

Decimals to percents

$1.25 \times 100\% = 125\%$

Percents to decimals

$250\% = 250 \div 100 = 2.50$

Addition and subtraction

a)
$$
\begin{array}{r}
4.53 \\
+ \;.45 \\
\hline
4.98
\end{array}
$$

b)
$$
\begin{array}{r}
6.0 \\
- 3.8 \\
\hline
2.2
\end{array}
$$

Multiplication

$$
\begin{array}{r}
5.6 \\
\times \; 0.1 \\
\hline
56
\end{array}
\text{ (2 decimals) } \Rightarrow 0.56
$$

Division

$$0.05\,\overline{)14.25} \;=\; 5\,\overline{)1425}^{\;285}$$

Ordering

Compare the digits in the different places: 0.00... is the smallest.

1.2
0.876
0.00999   In order: 0.00999, 0.876, 1.2

DECIMAL SYSTEM

6 is in the hundreds place, 7 in the ones, 8 in the tenths and 2 in the hundredths place. The values of the digits are:

$600, 7, \frac{8}{10}, \frac{2}{100}$

DISTANCE

$13 - 1 = 12, 12^2 = 144; \quad 10 - 5 = 5, 5^2 = 25$

$$\sqrt{144 + 25} = \sqrt{169} = 13$$

DISTRIBUTIVE PRINCIPLE (LAW)

$(100 - 1)15 = 1500 - 15 = 1485$

DIVISIBILITY RULES

a)   112, 114   b)   111, 114

EQUATION

b and c

EVALUATE

a) $3 + 2 \times 4 = 3 + 8 = 11$
b) $3(2)^2 + 4(2) + 5 = 12 + 8 + 5 = 25$

EXPANDED FORM

$5 \times 10{,}000 + 3 \times 100 + 9 \times 10 + 1$ or
$5 \times 10^4 + 3 \times 10^2 + 9 \times 10 + 1$

EXPONENT

Natural number

a) $3^4 = 3 \times 3 \times 3 \times 3 = 9 \times 9 = 81$
b) $4^3 = 4 \times 4 \times 4 = 64$

Zero 1

Negative number $\frac{1}{2^5}$ or $\frac{1}{32}$

Fraction $\sqrt{49}$

Addition/subtraction

a) $11x^2$ b) $2a^2$ c) $9 - 3 = 6$
Note: There is no shortcut in addition/subtraction.

Multiplication

$5^2 a^3 \cdot 5^6 a^7 = 5^8 a^{10}$ or $390{,}625\, a^{10}$ (Use a calculator!)

Division

$42 \div 7 = 6, x^2 \div x^2 = 1, y^7 \div y^3 = y^4$ Answer: $6y^4$

Powers

$2^6 = 64;\ 8^2 = 64$
$2^3 5^3 = 8 \times 125 = 1000;\ 10^3 = 1000$

FACTOR TREE

```
    24
    / \
  2   12
      / \
     2   6
         / \
        2   3
```

FACTORING (FACTORIZATION)

Prime factors

$50 = 2 \times 25 = 2 \times 5 \times 5$

Factor completely: Greatest common factor

$3x(x^3 + 2x^2 + 3x - 7)$

Factor a polynomial

Step 1   a) $6x(x + 2y)$ b) $10xy(y - 2x)$

Step 2   Difference of squares

     a) $(3x - 4)(3x + 4)$ b) $3(x - 2)(x + 2)$

     Difference of cubes

     a) $(x - 4)(x^2 + 4x + 16)$

     b) $8x^3 - 64 = 8(x^3 - 8) = 8(x^3 - 2^3)$
$$= 8(x - 2)(x^2 + 2x + 4)$$

     Sum of cubes

     $8x^3 + 27 = (2x)^3 + 3^3 = (2x + 3)(4x^2 - 6x + 9)$

     Trinomials

     a) $x^2 + 8x + 15 = (x + 3)(x + 5)$;
        $3 + 5 = 8$ and $3(5) = 15$

     b) $x^2 - 2x - 15 = (x - 5)(x + 3)$;
        $-5 + 3 = -2$ and $-5(3) = -15$

     Coefficient of $x^2 \neq 1$

     a) $3x^2 + 7x + 2 = (3x + 1)(x + 2)$

     Guess 1 and 2; then check using FOIL.

     b) $3x^2 + 5x - 2 = (3x - 1)(x + 2)$

     Guess 2 and –1; then check using FOIL.

FOIL

     a) $(x - 3)(x + 3) = x^2 \, (F) + 3x(O) - 3x(I) - 9(L) = x^2 - 9$

     b) $(2x - 5)(3x + 4) = 6x^2 + 8x - 15x - 20 = 6x^2 - 7x - 20$

FRACTIONS

Addition and subtraction

a) $\dfrac{4}{8} = \dfrac{1}{2}$

b) $6\dfrac{5}{5} = 7$

Different denominators

a) $\frac{2}{5} + \frac{3}{10} = \frac{4}{10} + \frac{3}{10} = \frac{7}{10}$

b) $\frac{5}{9} - \frac{1}{6} = \frac{10}{18} - \frac{3}{18} = \frac{7}{18}$

Borrowing

a) $1 - \frac{3}{5} = \frac{5}{5} - \frac{3}{5} = \frac{2}{5}$

b) $4\frac{1}{3} - 2\frac{2}{3} = 3\frac{4}{3} - 2\frac{2}{3} = 1\frac{2}{3}$

Multiplication

a) $\frac{1}{7} \times \frac{2}{7} = \frac{2}{49}$

b) $1\frac{1}{2} \times 4\frac{2}{3} = \frac{3}{2} \times \frac{14}{3} = 7$

Division

a) $\frac{3}{7} \div \frac{1}{7} = \frac{3}{7} \times \frac{7}{1} = 3$

b) $3\frac{1}{3} \div 2\frac{1}{2} = \frac{10}{3} \div \frac{5}{2} = \frac{10}{3} \times \frac{2}{5} = \frac{4}{3} = 1\frac{1}{3}$

Powers

a) $\left(\frac{1}{2}\right)^5 = \frac{1^5}{2^5} = \frac{1}{32}$

b) $\left(2\frac{3}{5}\right)^3 = \left(\frac{13}{5}\right)^3 = \frac{2197}{125} = 17\frac{72}{125}$

Ordering

a) $\frac{2}{3} = \frac{26}{39}$ $\frac{8}{13} = \frac{24}{39}$ $\frac{8}{13}$ is smaller

b) $\frac{1}{7} = \frac{13}{91}$ $\frac{2}{13} = \frac{14}{91}$ $\frac{1}{7}$ is smaller

FUNCTION

  a and *b*

GRAPHING

Possible points:

(2,3), (3,2), (0,5)

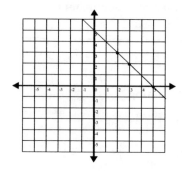

GREATER THAN

2 > 0

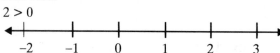

GREATEST COMMON FACTOR (GCF)

$20 = 2 \times 2 \times 5$

$50 = 2 \times 5 \times 5$ $2 \times 5 = 10$ is the GCF

GROUPING SYMBOLS

$12 - \{20 - [7 + (10 - 8)]\} = 12 - \{20 - [7 + 2]\}$
$$= 12 - \{20 - 9\} = 12 - 11 = 1$$

HECTO

0.1 hg

INDEX OF ROOTS

a) 5   *b*) 9   *c*) 2

INEQUALITIES

5 > 2

Operations

Addition and subtraction: $2 < 9, 2 + 4 < 9 + 4, 6 < 13$

Multiplication: $3 < 5, 3 \times 4 = 12, 5 \times 4 = 20, \ 12 < 20$
$$3 < 5, 3(-4) = -12, 5(-4) = -20, -12 > -20$$

INTEGERS

Operations

Addition:

a) $-1 + (-6)$ Add absolute values and keep the sign.

Answer -7

b) $-9 + 7$ (Subtract absolute values; keep sign of the number with the highest absolute value.) Answer: -2

Subtraction:

a) $-8 - 4$ (Change subtraction to addition of the opposite.)
$-8 + (-4) = -12$;

b) $-8 - (-4) = -8 + 4 = -4$

Multiplication

a) $-4(9)$ (Multiply absolute values. Signs are different so the product is negative.) Answer: -36

b) $(-4)(-9)$ (Multiply absolute values. Signs are the same so the product is positive.) Answer: 36

Multiplication of two or more signed numbers

a) $4(-6)(10)$ (Multiply absolute values. One negative sign, product is negative.) Answer: -240

b) $(-4)(-6)(10)$ (2 negative signs; the product is positive.)

Answer: 240

Division

a) $45 \div (-5)$ (Divide absolute values. Signs are different so the quotient is negative.) Answer: -9

b) $-45 \div (-5)$ (Divide absolute values. Signs are the same so the quotient is positive.) Answer: 9

Powers

a) $-(-2)^2 = -(4)$ Answer: -4

b) $(-2)^3 = (-8)$ Answer: -8

INTERCEPTS

$y = 0$, x–intercept $= -3$; $x = 0$, y–intercept $= 3$

INTEREST

a) $\$4,000 \times 2\% \times 10 = \$800$ Interest $= \$800$

b) $\$4,000(1 + \frac{2\%}{12})^{120} = \$4884.80$
$\$4,884.80 - \$4,000 = \$884.80$ Interest $= \$884.80$

INVERSE

    a) $-4 + 4 = 0$ *b*) $-\frac{1}{4}$

INVERT

    a) 5   *b*) $-\frac{1}{7}$

IRRATIONAL NUMBERS

    c

KILO

    0.1 km

LEAST COMMON DENOMINATOR (LCD)

    12, 24, 36, 48,...
    18, 36, ...   LCD = 36

LEAST COMMON MULTIPLE (LCM)

    16, 32, 48, 64, 80, 96, 112, 128, 144,...
    18, 36, 54, 72, 90, 108, 126, 144,...   LCM = 144

    Alternate method: $16 = 2^4, 18 = 2 \times 3^2$
                    LCM $= 2^4 \times 3^2 = 16 \times 9 = 144$

LESS THAN

    $-10 < -6$

LIKE TERMS

    $2ax^2$ and $7ax^2$

LITER

    250 cl

LONG DIVISION

    1)

$$\begin{array}{r} 52 \\ 7\overline{)364} \\ -\underline{35} \\ 14 \\ -\underline{14} \end{array}$$

    2)

$$\begin{array}{r} x + 3 \\ x + 2 \overline{)x^2 + 5x + 6} \\ -\underline{x^2 - 2x} \\ 3x + 6 \\ -\underline{3x - 6} \end{array}$$

MAGNITUDE

    7

Mean

$$\frac{(1+2+3+3+4+5)}{6} = 3$$

Median

3 (middle number)

Meter

$1.5 \times 100 = 150$ cm

Metric system

Length	*a*)	$15/10 = 1.5$;	1.5 m
	b)	$0.4 \times 100 = 40$;	40 cm
Weight (mass)	*a*)	$500/1000 = 0.5$;	0.5 kg
	b)	$1 \times 100 = 100$;	100 g
Volume (liquid)	*a*)	$0.6 \times 100 = 60$;	60 dl
	b)	$750/1000 = 0.75$;	0.75 l
Volume (solid)	*a*)	$0.005 \times 1,000,000 = 5000$;	5000 cm³
	b)	$1.5 \times 1000 = 1500$;	1500 mm³

Volume (conversion)   5 ml (ml and cc are the same.)

Area $2 \times 100 = 200$;   200 cm²

Conversion metric/customary

a)   100 m = 10,000 cm = 10,000/2.54 in = 3937 in
          = 3937/12 ft = 328 ft = 328/3 yards = 109 yards

b)   100 g = 100/454 lbs = 0.22 lbs = 0.22 × 16 oz = 3.5 oz

Mixture Problems

10 60-cent stamps and 110 34-cent stamps

Mode

8

Monomials

Operations

Addition and subtraction	$3ab$
Multiplication	$12x^2y^4$
Division	$4x^2y^4$

Powers

$$(5a^3b)^3 = 5^3 a^9 b^3 = 125a^9b^3$$

MOTION (RATE) PROBLEMS

	Down	Up
r	$x + y$	$x - y$
t	3 h	6 h
d	24 mi	24 mi

Equations

$(x + y)3 = 24$
$(x - y)6 = 24$

Solution

$x + y = 8$
$\underline{x - y = 4}$
$2x = 12$
$x = 6, y = 2$

Answer: 6 mph in still water; 2 mph current

MULTIPLE

8, 16, 24, 32, 40, 48

NEGATIVE EXPONENTS

$$\frac{3^2}{2} = \frac{9}{2} = 4\frac{1}{2}$$

NUMBER PROBLEMS

Numbers are $x, x + 1, x + 2$;

$$x + x + 1 + x + 2 = 33$$
$$3x + 3 = 33$$
$$x = 10$$

The numbers are 10, 11, 12.

OPPOSITES

0

ORDER OF OPERATIONS

a) $15 \div 5(3) = 3(3) = 9$; Left to right

b) $\dfrac{5 \times 3^2 + 6}{3 \times 5 + 2} = \dfrac{5 \times 9 + 6}{15 + 2} = \dfrac{45 + 6}{17} = \dfrac{51}{17} = 3$

ORDINATE

9

PARENTHESES

$$50 - 2(3(2(5 - 4) + 6))$$

PERCENT

Conversions

Percents into decimals $25\% = 25 \div 100 = 0.25$

Percents into fractions $25\% = 25 \div 100 = \frac{1}{4}$

Numbers into percents

a) $0.125 = 0.125 \times 100\% = 12.5\%$

b) $\frac{1}{8} = \frac{1}{8} \times 100\% = \frac{100}{8}\% = 12.5\%$

Problem solving

By use of proportions:

Type 1 $\frac{N}{100} = \frac{20}{25}$ $25N = 2000$ $N = 80$ or 80%

Type 2 $\frac{50}{100} = \frac{3}{N}$ $50N = 300$ $N = 6$

Type 3 $\frac{30}{100} = \frac{N}{500}$ $100N = 15000$ $N = 150$

By arithmetic:

Type 1 $\frac{20}{25} \times 100\% = 80\%$

Type 2 $\frac{3}{50\%} = \frac{3}{0.5} = 6$

Type 3 $30\% \times 500 = 150$

By direct translation into algebra:

Type 1 $x(25) = 20$ $x = 0.80$ or 80%
Type 2 $50\%x = 3$ $x = 6$
Type 3 $x = 30\% (500)$
        $x = 150$

Percents added 106% of price $= 106$
                    The original price was \$100

PERFECT CUBES

Numbers: 27 (3^3), 125 (5^3)
Expressions: $x^3 + 9x^2 + 27x + 27$
              $a = x, b = 3, 3a^2b = 9x^2; 3ab^2 = 27x$
              Insert in formula: $(x + 3)^3$

PERFECT SQUARES

Numbers   4, 16
Expressions $a = x, 2ab = 8x, b = 4$ Insert in formula: $(x + 4)^2$

PERIMETER

8 inches

PLACE VALUE

Whole numbers	700
Decimals	7 thousandths

PLOTTING POINTS

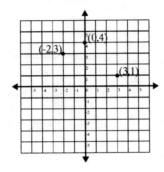

POINT-SLOPE FORM

$$y - 1 = 1(x - 1) \qquad y = x$$

POLYNOMIALS

Polynomials in one variable

5

Operations

Subtraction

$$
\begin{aligned}
4x^2 + 3x - 1 &= 4x^2 + 3x - 1 \\
-(x^2 - 5x + 1) &= \underline{-x^2 + 5x - 1} \\
& \quad\ \ 3x^2 + 8x - 2
\end{aligned}
$$

Multiplication

1. $2a^2b^3(5a^3) = 10a^5b^3$
2. $6x^2y^3(2x^3 + xy) = 12x^5y^3 + 6x^3y^4$
   Use the distributive law.
3. $(x + 2)(x + 2) = x^2 + 2x + 2x + 4 = x^2 + 4x + 4$
   (FOIL)
4. $(x + y + 5)(x - y + 2) =$
   $x^2 - xy + 2x + xy - y^2 + 2y + 5x - 5y + 10 =$
   $x^2 + 7x - y^2 - 3y + 10$

Division

1. $\dfrac{3a+6}{3} = \dfrac{3a}{3} + \dfrac{6}{3} = a + 2$

$$\begin{array}{r} x+3 \\ x+2 \overline{\smash{\big)}\ x^2+5x+6} \\ \underline{-x^2-2x} \\ 3x+6 \\ \underline{-3x-6} \end{array}$$

2.

POWERS OF 10

Operations

a) $0.5 \times 10^{-2} = 0.005$
(Move the decimal point two steps to the left.)

b) $0.5 \div 10^{-2} = 50$
(Move the decimal point two steps to the right.)

PRIME FACTOR

2, 5

PRIME FACTORIZATION

$2 \times 2 \times 5$

PRIME NUMBER

Yes

PRINCIPAL SQUARE ROOT

5

PROBABILITY

There are 15 yellow out of a total of 50 jellybeans. The probability of getting a yellow is $\frac{15}{50}$ or $\frac{3}{10}$.

PYTHAGOREAN THEOREM

$(5)^2 + (12)^2 = 25 + 144 = 169 = (13)^2 \qquad c = 13$

PYTHAGOREAN TRIPLETS

$(6)^2 + (8)^2 = 36 + 64 = 100 = (10)^2$ 6, 8, 10 is a triplet.

$(8)^2 + (15)^2 = 64 + 225 = 289 = (17)^2$ 8, 15, 17 is a triplet.

QUADRANTS

Negative

QUADRATIC EQUATION

a) $x^2 + 2x - 3 = 0$
      $(x + 3)(x - 1) = 0$
           $x_1 = -3; \ x_2 = 1$

b) $a = 1, b = 2, c = -3$

$$x = \frac{-2 \pm \sqrt{4 + 4(1)(3)}}{2(1)}$$

$$x = \frac{-2 \pm 4}{2} \qquad x_1 = -3; \ x_2 = 1$$

c)

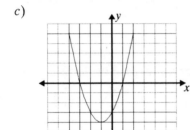

Solution: $x_1 = -3; \ x_2 = 1$

RADICAL

Operations

Addition: $7\sqrt[3]{4}$

Multiplication and division:

a) $\sqrt[5]{4} \times \sqrt[5]{8} = \sqrt[5]{32} = \sqrt[5]{2^5} = 2;$

b) $\dfrac{\sqrt[3]{9}}{\sqrt[3]{3}} = \sqrt[3]{\dfrac{9}{3}} = \sqrt[3]{3}$

RADICAL EQUATIONS

$$\sqrt{x+2} = x$$

$$x + 2 = x^2 \Rightarrow (x + 1)(x - 2) = 0 \qquad x = -1; \ x = 2$$

Check: $x = -1$: $\sqrt{-1+2} = 1$ reject

$x = 2$: $\sqrt{2+2} = \sqrt{4} = 2$

Answer: $x = 2$; reject $x = -1$

RATE PROBLEMS

$220 = 55x \Rightarrow x = 4$ Answer: 4 hours

RATIO

$\dfrac{15}{18} = 5:6$

RATIO AND PROPORTION PROBLEMS

Ratio

Boys: $3x$ Girls: $4x$ $3x + 4x = 28$

$$7x = 28$$

$$x = 4 \quad 4x = 16 \quad \text{Answer:16 girls}$$

Proportion

$$\frac{4}{150} = \frac{x}{225}$$
$$4(225) = 150x$$
$$x = 4(225)/150$$
$$x = 6$$

Answer: 6 days

RATIONAL EQUATIONS

$$\frac{1}{2} = \frac{1}{x} + \frac{1}{6} \quad \text{LCD} = 6x \quad 3x = 6 + x$$

$$x = 3$$

RATIONAL EXPRESSION

Operations

Reducing $\dfrac{x^2y + xy^2}{x + y} = \dfrac{xy(x + y)}{x + y} = xy$

Addition and subtraction

a) $\dfrac{3x}{2y^2} + \dfrac{1}{4xy} = \dfrac{6x^2}{4xy^2} + \dfrac{y}{4xy^2} = \dfrac{6x^2 + y}{4xy^2}$ (LCD $= 4xy^2$)

b) $\dfrac{3}{2xy^2} - \dfrac{1}{4x^2y} = \dfrac{6x}{4x^2y^2} - \dfrac{y}{4x^2y^2} = \dfrac{6x - y}{4x^2y^2}$

Multiplication and division

a) $\dfrac{3x^2}{2y} \div \dfrac{3x}{4y^3} = \dfrac{3x^2}{2y} \times \dfrac{4y^3}{3x} = 2xy^2$

b) $\dfrac{x^2 + 2x}{x} \times \dfrac{(x-2)^2}{x^2 - 4} = \dfrac{x(x+2)(x-2)(x-2)}{x(x-2)(x+2)} = x - 2$

RATIONAL NUMBERS

$$7 = \frac{7}{1}$$

Rationalizing

Monomial $\dfrac{5}{\sqrt{5}} = \dfrac{5\sqrt{5}}{\sqrt{5}\sqrt{5}} = \dfrac{5\sqrt{5}}{5} = \sqrt{5}$

Binomial $\dfrac{2}{2+\sqrt{2}} = \dfrac{2}{2+\sqrt{2}} \times \dfrac{2-\sqrt{2}}{2-\sqrt{2}} = \dfrac{2(2-\sqrt{2})}{4-2} = 2 - \sqrt{2}$

Reading numbers

Whole numbers: One hundred five thousand two hundred six

Decimal numbers: Twelve and twenty-five thousandths

Real numbers

The minus sign is <u>outside</u> the radical sign.

Thus $-(\sqrt{4}) = -(2) = -2$

Rectangle

Yes

Reducing fractions

a) $\dfrac{10}{15} = \dfrac{2}{3}$

b) $\dfrac{3x^2y^5}{6xy^6} = \dfrac{x}{2y}$

Repeating decimals

63

Rhombus

Square

Root

Equations   No; $3 - 3 = 0$, not 1

Exponential notation $\sqrt[3]{64} = \sqrt[3]{4^3} = 4$

Rounding

Whole numbers $5\underline{9},|830$ Add 1 to 9; add zeroes to show place value: 60,000

Decimals $24.36\underline{8}\,|42$ Disregard 42; Answer: 24.368

Satisfy an equation

$2(1) + 1 = 2 + 1 = 3$

SCALES

SCIENTIFIC NOTATION

$54{,}690 = 5.469 \times 10^4$ The decimal point was moved 4 steps.

SIMPLIFY

$$2ab^3(5a^2b^4) = 2(5)a^{1+2}b^{3+4} = 10a^3b^7$$

SIMULTANEOUS EQUATIONS

Method 1:

$2x + 3y = 7$ Multiply by 3: $6x + 9y = 21$
$3x + 2y = 8$ Multiply by –2: $-6x - 4y = -16$
$$5y = 5 \quad y = 1$$
$$2x + 3(1) = 7 \quad x = 2$$

Method 2:

$$x + y = 5$$
$$x - y = 3$$
Solve for x: $x = y + 3$
Replace: $(y + 3) + y = 5$
$$2y = 2$$
$$y = 1 \qquad x + 1 = 5 \qquad x = 4$$

Solve by Method 1:

$$x + 2y = 5$$
$$x - y = 2$$
Subtract: $3y = 3$
$$y = 1 \qquad x - 1 = 2 \qquad x = 3$$

Solve by Method 2:

$$x + 2y = 5$$
$$x - y = 2$$
Solve for x: $x = y + 2$
Substitute: $y + 2 + 2y = 5$
$$3y = 3 \qquad y = 1 \qquad x = 3$$

Solve by Method 3:

$$x + 2y = 5$$
$$x - y = 2$$
$$x = 3$$
$$y = 1$$

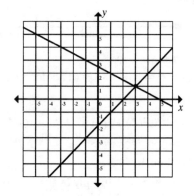

Slope

a) $m = \dfrac{2-0}{3-1} = \dfrac{2}{2} = 1$

b) $y = x + 3$ $\qquad m = 1$

Slope-intercept form

$$y = mx + b; m = 3, b = 2; \quad \text{Equation: } y = 3x + 2$$

Solving linear equations

Whole numbers

a)
$$\begin{aligned} 5x + 3 &= 2x + 9 \\ -2x - 3 &= -2x - 3 \\ \hline 3x &= 6 \qquad x = 2 \end{aligned}$$

b)
$$\begin{aligned} 4 + 8x &= 36 \\ -4 \qquad &\quad -4 \\ \hline 8x &= 32 \qquad x = 4 \end{aligned}$$

c) $\dfrac{x}{5} = 2$ $\qquad$ Multiply both sides by $5: x = 10$

Fractions

$\dfrac{x}{3} - \dfrac{x}{5} = 2$ $\quad$ LCD$=15$ $\qquad$ Multiply both sides by 15:

$5x - 3x = 30$

$\qquad 2x = 30$ $\qquad x = 15$

Decimals

$1x - 0.5x = 0.14 + 0.3x$ Multiply both sides by 100:
$100x - 50x = 14 + 30x$
$20x = 14$ $x = 0.7$

General

a) $5x + 3 = 2x + 9$
    $3x = 6$ $x = 2$

b) $7x - 3 = 25$
    $\underline{+3 \quad +3}$
    $7x = 28$ $x = 4$

c) $\frac{x}{3} = 1$ Multiply both sides by 3: $x = 3$

d) $\frac{x}{5} + \frac{x}{15} = 4$ Multiply both sides by 15:
    $3x + x = 60$
    $4x = 60$ $x = 15$

e) $x - 0.15x = 2.1 + 0.15x$ Multiply both sides by 100:
    $100x - 15x = 210 + 15x$
    $70x = 210$ $x = 3$

SQUARE

$$(3x - 2)^2 = (3x)^2 - 12x + 4 = 9x^2 - 12x + 4$$

SQUARE ROOT

13 (guess and multiply back)

SUBSTITUTE

$3x + 2y^2$ $x = 3$ and $y = 4$ $3(3) + 2(16) = 41$

TEMPERATURE

a) Double 25; add 30 = 80

    Formula: $\frac{9}{5}(25) + 32 = 45 + 32 = 77$
    Answer: $80°F, 77°F$

b) Subtract 30, divide by 2: $80 - 30 = 50$ $\frac{50}{2} = 25$

    Formula: $\frac{5}{9}(80 - 32) = \frac{5}{9}(48) = 26.6...$
    Answer: $25°C, 27°C$

UNIT

99¢ for 3 oranges. Each costs 33¢ which is the unit price.

WHOLE NUMBERS

A fraction or a decimal

WORK PROBLEMS

	Rate of work	Time	Part of task
Lisa	$\frac{1}{45}$	x min.	$\frac{x}{45}$
Brit	$\frac{1}{30}$	x min.	$\frac{x}{30}$

$\frac{x}{45} + \frac{x}{30} = 1$ LCD = 90

$2x + 3x = 90$

$5x = 90$

$x = 18$

Answer: 18 minutes

X-INTERCEPT

$y = 0,$ $3x - 9 = 0$

$x = 3$ The x-intercept is 3.

Y-INTERCEPT

$x = 0,$ $y = -6$ The y-intercept is -6.

ZERO

Operations

Division: Error

Power: $2^0 = 1$ $3^0 = 1$ $1 \times 1 = 1$ Answer: 1

ABOUT THE AUTHOR

Brita Immergut taught mathematics for 30 years in middle schools, high schools, and colleges. She was a Professor of Mathematics at LaGuardia Community College of the City University of New York. She has conducted workshops and taught courses for math-anxious adults at schools and organizations. Professor Immergut received an M.S. in mathematics, physics, and chemistry from Uppsala University in Sweden and an Ed.D. in mathematics education from Teachers College, Columbia University. She is the co-author of two textbooks for adults: *Arithmetic and Algebra...Again* and *An Introduction to Algebra: A workbook for Reading, Writing and Thinking about Mathematics.*